Oh, My Gosh, We're Pregnant!

Book One of

The Parents' Survival Kit

BY

PAUL PEEBLES, M.D.

The following, covering the time of pregnancy and delivery, is the first book in the series entitled *The Parents' Survival Kit*.

Published by
Pediatric Care Publications
c/o The Pediatric Care Center
Old Georgetown Road Manor House
5612 Spruce Tree Avenue
Bethesda, Maryland 20814, USA

photographs by Karin Kristine Ottesen, Paul Peebles, and Lisa Helfer; cartoons by Sari Werner; graphics by Kathy Peterson

SPECIAL THANKS
to
Grafik Communications, Ltd. of Alexandria, Virginia for cover design and layout and Children's National Medical Center of Washington, D.C. for photos on attachment in Neonatal Intensive Care Unit and to the parents who permitted photography of themselves and their children.

Also special thanks to my daughter Rebecka for publication advice, my son Gustav for copy-editing, and my wife Inger for ever-present support and help.

Library of Congress Catalog Card Number
Peebles, Paul
    Oh, My Gosh, We're Pregnant! / by Paul Peebles, M.D.-1st ed.

1. Pregnancy 2. Childbirth	includes index
3. Postnatal Care 4. Relationships	includes illustrations
	ISBN 0-9660853-0-2

Library of Congress Catalog Card Number: 97-92729

Printed in the United States of America

TABLE OF CONTENTS

LIST OF ANECDOTES

DEDICATION

During his life time Dr. George Khoury, his wife, and children became a part of our family. Dr. Khoury, a paragon of scientific and personal integrity, gave of himself to his friends and to humanity by accomplishing major achievements in biomedical research. ■ This book is written in special tribute to his love for his children Lisa and David who along with the rest of his family, friends, and the world of science were cheated by his premature death. His life-loving smile, cheerful optimism, and parting counsel, "Never lose your perspective on the really important things in life," will remain in our hearts. ■

What Is This Book About?

"HAVING A BABY IS A REAL SCREAM!"
JOAN RIVERS

Preventive Psychiatry. That's what this book (and the rest of the series) is about.

There is no elegant way to deliver. And pregnancy is more often more distorting than pleasant, both for a mother and a father. The first few years receives mixed review with rewards, deprivations, and challenges. Babies do not come with an owner's manual, nor are they always "user friendly," not to mention that there is a "no return" policy.

We parents, after the arrival of that new infant, are often in turmoil and desperate to stay afloat. Understandably, we want to do things for ourselves, but staying on our own two feet is not easy. Others, lots of them, offer advice — more often than not conflicting — and we feel torn in the attempt to do what is right. We are foggy with exhaustion. Our life of intimacy as husband and wife is often totally lost in the consumption of the self-sacrificing moment.

So…how do we survive this emotional vortex…and enjoy it?

That is also what this book is about.

THE METHODS FOR SURVIVAL

To gain control, it is helpful to first understand where we as parents are in our own development and to seek to understand from whence we have come. To cope as parents, it is key that we understand our own feelings. Only then can we begin to manage them.

Second, it is necessary to try to figure out our individual infant's temperament, and to ascertain where he is at in terms of his own particular development. Then we will know what to expect. What we wish for or expect may differ considerably from what we get.

Others also react to the arrival of this newborn. Family, friends, and others not only do things for us…but to us. Thus, third, to learn how their behavior may impact us allows us to develop strategies for surviving these interactions.

1

Finally, after acquiring some idea of where we and our infant are at and what others reacting to this rite of passage are doing to us, we can develop some concepts for coping and problem solving.

THE STRUCTURE OF THE BOOK AND SERIES

Pregnancy and delivery are presented in this book. The stories and ideas will be presented chronologically. The first six weeks and the first year and thereafter will be covered in later books. In this book four sections will be presented, (1) The Psychological Development of Today's Parents, (2) The Genesis of the Human Infant's Psyche, (3) The Reactions of Others, and (4) Concepts for Coping. However, the reader will notice that certain themes will weave throughout the book. The Intruder Complex, The Intimacy Drive, Separation Fears, The Instinct for Happiness, and Rescue Versus Empathy are examples of repetitive themes that continue despite the age of the child and the stage of the parents. These themes are enduring in the lives of all families.

Additionally, a reader may see, and be living a problem described in the sections on the development of the parents or child and reactions of others, but be frustrated that the initial description appears to offer no answer. Don't despair. The answers are given separately in the section called Coping Concepts.

Certain anecdotes will be related in a fractured fashion. The part of the story that relates to the period covered by the specific chapter or part of the book will be told, and the remaining parts will be forthcoming in later chronologically appropriate parts or chapters of books to follow. Should a reader wish to follow an anecdote from beginning to end, the appropriate pages can be found in the list of anecdotes.

WHY WRITE THIS BOOK SERIES?

New data from Sweden reveal that over there half of all marital separations are occurring within one year after the arrival of the first born. It is clear to this author, a pediatrician with thirty years of experience, that the arrival of children is a major stress factor in marriage. How's that for a truism?

This author is also convinced from experience that The Intruder Complex (a concept described for the first time in this book series) is the major cause of divorce in parents who were doing perfectly fine prior to pregnancy. And whether we like to hear it or not while anticipating the joyful arrival of this wonderful baby, divorce still is averaging around 50% in the USA; it is additionally estimated that six out of ten children will spend some part of their growing years in a single parent home! But perhaps the most chilling statistic is that two-thirds of the divorces occur within the first six years after the birth of the first child.

We can either grow from or succumb to stress. This book series is intended as assistance for managing the ordinary, although stressful problems confronting good parents with healthy kids. It is this author's wish that the dissection of ourselves, the infant, and the events surrounding this new arrival will make us parents feel whole again. That, along with the development of coping concepts, has proven immensely helpful to parents who have taken the course upon which these books are based.

For over twenty years I have explored these concepts in group sessions and classes with parents. Hence, the origin of these concepts came from parents. They were the ones who felt these topics essential. And it was they who sought, and gave, information regarding these aspects of learning about and dealing with ourselves and our infants.

The survival of more parents and children as intact families is the goal of this series. Hopefully it will decrease the mystery and enhance the enjoyment of the amazing and unbelievably rapid process of our and our infant's development in the early years of life.

Clearly many child care and parenting books and magazines are out there. So what sets this book series apart from the rest?

First, sophisticated child, and parent, developmental issues are discussed, but hopefully so that all will understand them.

Second, no other book discusses the important novel issues presented in this series with regards to parents' emotional development. All books before have concentrated on the child's, perhaps also the mother's, but never the father's emotional development. Nor have they focused on the influence of the parents' interactions together on their own and the child's development.

Most important, this book and its series helps parents to survive, to stay afloat, to cope, and to master the challenges. Other books and magazines may offer advice, admonitions on what to do and not to do. Other books more often are simply descriptive insightful narratives on child development. This book series proffers concepts for coping which can be individualized. It helps parents toward self-mastery without a preprogrammed format. It gives parents dignity. This book is for survival…and survival with pride and fun.

Finally the series is highly illustrative in nature and contains numerous graphics, cartoons, and photographs. This feature helps make complex developmental issues easily understood.

"I CAN'T BELIEVE WE JUST HAD HER ONE YEAR AGO…IT GOES WAY TOO FAST."

3

He certainly is a presence between you:
The Beginning of The Intruder Complex.

Pregnancy: Preparation for The Rite

"I DIDN'T GROW UP UNTIL I HAD A KID."
BILLY JOEL, 1990

In the law, a woman, even a fourteen year old, who has given birth to a baby is considered an adult. A teenager without child may not be able to give permission for her own surgery. Yet, if she has delivered a child, in the law she can give permission both for herself and that child.

In our society marriage is the penultimate step for a woman into adulthood, and having a baby is the ultimate required to stand in the ranks of women fulfilled, accomplished, separate, and standing on their own two feet. Some very young women may want to have a child to be "grown-up." Other professionally accomplished older women who have delayed pregnancy may feel "the biological clock running out." Having a child becomes the ultimate accomplishment of womanhood. Some may disagree with these statements, or wish that they were not true. However, I would argue that whatever any of us think should be the case, these are nonetheless the operating codes of our current society.

Having a baby is as much, if not more so, a rite of passage as confirmation and bar mitzvah, graduation from college, and marriage. Parents, relatives, and friends behave as if delivery is a rite of passage.

Parents want to stand on their own two feet. They want control. They want to do as much as they can for themselves, so that they themselves and others will view them as adults, and not just adults but hopefully as successful adults. Grandparents, other relatives, and friends celebrate.

Having a child is indeed a rite of passage, and becoming pregnant initiates this rite. And that fact alone explains a great deal of the human behavior of parents-to-be and those around them. As Billy Joel said, "I didn't grow up until I had a kid."

And, while parents grow up, others react. Some are supportive, respectful. Others, behaving almost enviously, seem to insist that you must suffer as they did. It is as if you must pledge the sorority/fraternity just as they have done. Why should you have it any better?!

5

Pregnancy and the Psychological Development of Today's Parents

THE DEVELOPMENT OF INTIMACY

Intimacy between couples is developed; it is not automatic. Just being married does not magically convey upon parents reflexive, instinctive intimacy…especially intimacy with strong bonds.

If you look back to the times you spent together before becoming pregnant, you went out. You saw movies together. You met for dinner. You discussed your jobs, what your boss did or did not do for you that day, what the workplace gossip was, and where your next vacation was going to be. You shared intimacies. You talked about yourselves and came to know each other more and more. You became close.

A time comes in the development of intimacy when you share with each other the things about which you are not so proud. You find you are not rejected, and you become even closer. You talk and share who you are with each other. You eventually, albeit not at all completely, get beyond or at least reach a balance regarding the issues of possessiveness and control of each other.

You become physically intimate. You walk hand-in-hand, arm-in-arm. You hug. You kiss. You touch…You make love. You form a close, warm, feeling, and knowing bond with each other. The firm commitment, the intimate closeness, and the love soften the fear of being tied down forsaking youthful freedom.

THE SEED GROWS

The Relentless Time Clock

Then, you opt for pregnancy and the clock ticks away. Suddenly there are decisions. Who will be the obstetrician? How do we find a good one? What will we do about our jobs? How do we prepare? Where do we go for child birth classes? How do we find a good pediatrician? Which child care books should we buy? How do we quickly find out how to have and handle a baby? Is the house or apartment large enough? Where are we going to put this kid?

Eager to Father

A graduate student, just recently married, expressed his strong desire to impregnate his wife, right away. Pondering his haste, I puzzled, "What's your hurry, how are you going to handle this economically?" He replied that he wanted "to make sure that everything works....I want to be sure that everything down there is put together right." This extremely conscious desire perilously disregarded his and his wife's financial situation and need for further education.

8

Suddenly Sissie's exclamation from *Gone With the Wind*, "I don't know nothin' 'bout birthin' babies, Miss Scarlet!" has more than humorous significance.

New concerns slowly permeate the barriers of old schedules and self-perceptions. A mother is never alone anymore. Parents wonder whether they can manage the expenses and responsibilities.

The ever-present time clock continues to tick away. It forces you to face unavoidable preparations. You suddenly find that you are no longer talking about yourselves, but are relentlessly commanded to discuss someone else – the baby!

Triumph and Exclusion

The Triumph

The successful fertilization of the student's wife *(Eager to Father)* resolved strong fears that he might be infertile, possibly not fully masculine.

Women have parallel fears. These fears that they may not be fully feminine erupt to the surface after multiple miscarriages or with infertility, when the need to pursue adoption might loom apparent.

Pregnant Together   Many fathers-to-be will experience the physical signs and symptoms of their wife's pregnancy. Some, rarely, develop vomiting during their wife's morning-sickness phase. More often, others anxiously gain weight throughout the pregnancy. Most fathers get these symptoms out of the added stress. Others do so unconsciously in imitation of their wives. While most often unconsciously felt, occasionally a father will consciously describe with lucidity the envy of his wife's power to bear a child.

Exclusion

The Beginning of The Intruder Complex

Once fertilization is accomplished, we fathers may begin feeling a sense of displacement and conscious jealousy. The irreversible pregnancy may begin threatening our identity as a husband, as previously the primary one in our wife's thoughts. We may tend to back off, avoiding being proud as potential fathers. As one father put it after going to parties, birthing classes, and baby showers, "The talk is forever about only this baby! Nobody knows even who I am or what I do!"

At child birth classes, prospective parents are taught breathing techniques to help during labor and delivery. Breast feeding is discussed. Child care books are introduced. These books discuss everything, but rarely the father. The couple will often meet or go out with other pregnant couples. The talk is incessantly about the coming babies. The father, who initially felt proud of his manhood, who fertilized this pregnancy, may now feel superfluous. He, even though involved and excited with anticipation, may also experience a foreboding sense of exclusion.

Fathers resent these exclusions and may envy the attention their wives are receiving. The pregnancy thus intrudes into their previously well-established life and relationship with their wives. This is the beginning of The Intruder Complex.

The anticipation of this intrusion may make some of us fathers reticent to even conceiving in the first place. As a father feels this, he may begin to have secret doubts and wonder if the pregnancy wasn't a mistake, even though outwardly he may declare he is ready and eager for fatherhood. He may become decidedly unexcited about this impending child. This is particularly true if the father himself grew up emotionally needy.

These feelings may be in contrast to those of the mother, whose task of delivery is yet to come, and who may be increasingly excited and anxious to see the baby delivered. She, at least toward the end, is certainly eager to see this child born and get this pregnancy over.

A father may then feel guilty and selfish for those negative, egocentric, and envious thoughts. He may wonder, "What is wrong with me?!" Arguments may result between expecting partners. Doubts may arise about the desirability of this pregnancy and becoming parents...or...even about the marriage.

Sex Life: Paradise Lost Another terribly important part of parents' life of intimacy together is our sexual life. In the beginning of the pregnancy, sex for parents wanes as they worry they may harm the fetus, or morning sickness may create enough nausea to interrupt any romantic feelings a mother or father may feel. As the pregnancy progresses, sex diminishes, especially during the last few months. And just before delivery, it has hit rock bottom!

The Feeling Is Felt A real sense evolves that this longed-for infant has truly intruded into the parents' life of intimacy, including their sex life. Less romance and concern with each other are felt intensely by parents. Their major dominating focus has become this new impending infant; he is center stage. That is The Intruder Complex. It is not just a feeling, it is a reality. The coming baby has intruded into their lives and has taken them hostage. The intruding pregnancy, this longed-for wonderful child, has taken over.

Territorial Intrusion This impending infant can even take over your space!

My Den?

We had just moved to Washington. Fortunately, we found an affordable house to rent. It was small but close to my work at the National Institutes of Health. It had three bedrooms, none of which were large. My wife and I took the largest. The next in size was just right as a small nursery for our 20-month-old daughter. The remaining room, the size of a walk-in closet, became my very first study room! We fixed it up with some nice curtains, put a door on bricks for a desk, and screwed some bookshelves into the wall over the desk. It was cozy, it was great!

Just after moving, we discovered we were expecting another child. Inevitably, my wife initiated the discussion as to where this new child was to sleep upon coming home after delivery. I argued for putting them both in the same room. However, our daughter's room was, to my chagrin, not large enough for two cribs. As much as I avoided thinking or talking about it, the solution became only too apparent. Out went the desk and the bookshelves, and in went the crib.

He was born. He was healthy, delightfully snugly. We brought him home to his very own room, my former study.

To give up that room was not at all easy for me! The children had not only intruded into my career and my relationship with my wife, but my new son had just taken over my very own room. I, I have to admit it, sulked...and ...reluctantly acquiesced...eventually. It was difficult. But he was truly worth it.

Wheezy

Before Wheezy was born her parents, Mr. and Mrs. Wishfergeld, had affluent aspirations. They were both employed and shared the conscious aspiration of attaining a financially successful life together. Their well-orchestrated ambitions were jolted when Mrs. Wishfergeld discovered she was four months pregnant, even though on the pill.

Both parents were depressed...and furious. Mr. Wishfergeld wanted an abortion. His wife disagreed crying, "Don't you want my baby?" She could not pursue the abortion. Wheezy was born, and conflicts ensued. (story to be continued in the next book.)

10

DIFFICULTIES DEVELOPING INTIMACY

The Stronger the Bond, the More Strain It Can Take

If parents have known each other for only a short time, then obviously fewer opportunities have occurred for the development of a strong life of intimacy together. Some older couples have gotten together late in life; feeling the biological clock ticking away, they decide to have children very soon after marriage. For other parents, barriers to intimacy exist that time has not resolved. Thus, the strength of parents' intimacy may be tenuous at the start. If that is the case, their intimacy can then be severely stressed by The Intruder Complex.

If the pregnancy is precipitous, unplanned, or unwanted by one or both parents, then the intrusion is resented even more. If exceptionally young parents receive an unanticipated infant, they may feel cheated out of the fun of their own adolescence. They may be completely unready for the responsibilities of child care.

A strong bond of intimacy, or the development of a strong bond of intimacy, is essential for surviving The Intruder Complex. So parents, if they wish to stay together under these circumstances, must make extra efforts to protect their life of intimacy. After delivery, if the relationship between husband and wife is to survive successfully, an even greater need exists for these parents to spend some time alone together.

The Intrusion of The Extended Family

When a young couple anticipates its first baby, the impending infant may not be the only intruder into the parents' life of intimacy. Some large extended families can be almost too much for new parents. Many families have close ties. Grandparents, uncles, and aunts may all live very close to each other, celebrating many cultural and religious holidays together.

These new parents may have to accept the intrusion of the entire wonderful family for months before and after delivery. It is particularly burdensome if the couple is young and has had only a few months together before the wife becomes pregnant. Pregnancy preoccupies their time and thoughts. Delivery automatically welcomes in all of the congratulating, interested, involved, and advice-giving relatives. A young couple may suddenly realize that the amount of time they have had for their own life of intimacy together has been unbelievably all too fleeting.

Taking on Responsibility

"Before if anything happened, it was just me and my wife, and she can survive without me. But now someone else is totally dependent upon my own success or failure."

LOSSES & FEARS

The Loss of The Old Self

Father's Fragile Strength Outwardly, a father may act self-confident, even macho. Yet he is often reluctant to accept that his life is changing as the pregnancy progresses. He has heard from many that things will never be the same. Feeling the need to escape, he may find himself working later hours or going out with his buddies rather than going home after work. Sometimes he may even come home

stumbling, mumbling from the drinks. He may frequent singles' bars by himself or indulge in anxious masturbation. The wife fears this behavior reflects disinterest in sex and herself, especially at a time when she feels less attractive.

A father may decide to change careers, or buy a new house, and move two weeks after the baby is born. It is as if some fathers may want to focus on something else rather than the concerns about accepting this new role. Some people find ways of setting up preoccupying crises to distract them from thinking about the upcoming event of a new person in the family. It is an escape to avoid thinking about something that might be even more upsetting and less manageable. It is not uncommon for significant marital problems, eventually leading to separation and divorce in some cases, to arise at this time.

We fathers are often worried about taking on the responsibilities in this new role. We are reluctant to change our preexisting roles. Worries about handling an infant come: "Will I be too strict or will I spoil him?" Most fathers share, but do not speak, the same worries of the mother.

We fathers like to feel successful. We feel proud thinking about becoming a father and having a nice family of our own. We begin to feel protective and possessive. However, the thought of a new infant in the house is also a challenge to those wishes and feelings. Anticipated demands for time and responsibility are keenly felt. A father, especially a career-oriented father, may feel burdened by concerns over financial problems, now that he may temporarily become the only

Gone are the days of the fancy-free young man.

No One Told Me

"No one told me before what it was going to be like. When they did, I thought, 'What did you do wrong – it's not going to be like that with me.'"

breadwinner in the family: "Before if anything happened, it was just me and my wife, and she can survive without me. But now someone else is totally dependent upon my own success or failure."

Although feeling proud, a father can feel burdened at the same time. He may now realize he can no longer afford to take real risks in his career. But, without some risk, there is far less gain. He may have less time and energy to pursue his career, and the fear of less success may worry him. Merely the anticipated thought of the necessity for time to help his wife and coming child begin to crowd into his tight life.

Some may resent the incessant new demands of their wife's pregnancy. It may be hard to manage and empathize with his wife's turmoils as she goes through the storm of increased hormones from pregnancy. A father may feel helpless when all attempts to calm her are unsuccessful. Anger, depression, and then guilty feelings may follow.

Gone are the days when he was unattached and free of responsibility. His sense of himself as a debonair young man is gone. He sees that self as an endangered species about to become extinct.

In contrast to the above, certain economically successful fathers may not experience some of these sentiments. Instead they may feel quite proud that they can pay for it all and not require their wife to return to the work force. They can then continue to pursue their careers and their wife will take care of all of the rest.

For Mothers

Denial of Difficulties   Mothers-to-be often feel dissociated from the difficulties they hear about from other mothers with newborns. One mother exclaimed, after having a child with a high-strung disposition, "No one told me before what it was going to be like. When they did, I thought, 'What did you do wrong – it's not going to be like that with me.'" The thought, or should I say wish, exists that all a mother has to do is to prepare everything right and there will be no difficulties. (*See Glossary for Wish Versus Reality*)

Glow Or Glum Gloom   A mother may want everything to go on as before, as if there are no changes in her life. She may want her career to be the same and her looks to go unchanged. She desires to remain in perfect control. Whether she will only live for her baby, or go on with her own life, letting the baby adapt to hers, are constantly pondered questions for all mothers. Just as the pregnancy and its changes created a substantial threat to the identity of the father, this pregnancy also threatens to destroy the mother's image of herself prior to her motherhood. "I want to keep on going in my career," one mother demanded.

This attempt to keep the status quo usually has few limits. It often applies to all areas of a mother's life: tennis, jogging, her life of intimacy with her husband including their sex life. The infant intrudes not only into her life of intimacy with her husband, but also into her sense and image of herself.

Some mothers describe a great joy in feeling and becoming pregnant by choice. They describe it as having a "glow." They are overwhelmingly proud and happy, they are at the beginning of this rite of passage.

Others, while they may be happy about the coming child, are not at all thrilled with feeling pregnant. During the first months little changes in the outward physical appearance of the body. Hormonally, however, much is going on. Most express happiness that the periods with their associated cramps are gone. The pain of endometriosis may be an illness of the past. But these problems may be replaced with "morning sickness," migraine headaches, vomiting (especially with the slightest whiff of an alcoholic beverage), sinusitis, and nasal stuffiness. Then comes the rapidly progressive weight gain and alteration in body size and shape. This is accompanied by the need to reluctantly eat for fear of the fetus's nutrition. And, finally, the facial mask of pregnancy (see Glossary) may overwhelm a pregnant mother's wish to keep her sense of self.

"I can't wait to get into my own clothes!"
Some may want to wear maternity clothes early, and others, less accepting of their changing body, may only reluctantly buy them. Many worry that their husband will find them less attractive. A mother may fish for compliments. When they don't come, she may find herself starting an argument by picking on a sensitive issue, or doing anything to get attention.

One pregnant mother complained, "This glow stuff is a myth. It's how I look and feel!

I feel fat and tired! And, it's wondering if I'll ever get back to the way I looked. It's the loss of my self image! It's awful!"

Toward the end of the pregnancy, a mother may fear it will never end. This trepidation is especially hard to bear if the pregnancy is prolonged beyond the due date.

A mother develops a growing awareness of the fetus's presence. His kick is felt or the infant's arms, legs, and head are seen on a sonogram. The child is real! As this reality evolves, the difficulties experienced may become more acceptable, even though not forgotten.

Will I Love Him? For most parents a fear about not being able to fall in love with a stranger looms large into their consciousness. "I was worried that I might not love this child. I never thought of myself as a mother."

13

These feelings emerge from the ambivalence aroused by the confrontation of wanting this new infant but, at the same time, being forced to give up a sense of an independent self.

The Loss of Invincibility

Then there are the fears about the infant's health. Will he be deformed or retarded? No effort to suppress them is effective. Even if the fears are quelled during the day, awful dreams wake you at night. The closer you are to the child care profession, the greater the worries. My wife worked for the Developmental Evaluation Clinic at Boston's Children's Hospital. Her greatest worry during pregnancy was having a retarded child. This worry stayed with us until our daughter talked.

Symptomatic of these fears is the amount and timing of the preparation for the baby by the parents. One expectant mother, a pediatrician working in a hospital caring on a daily basis for only the worst cases, worried to the extent that she dared not buy clothes and crib until late in the pregnancy. Then she did not open them, nor even unpack them, until the infant was born healthy. A wonderful joy and delight were felt by myself, not to mention them, watching her give directions over the phone from the hospital

to her husband who did not know where anything was at home. He had to hurriedly organize it all before she was discharged.

Fears Are Forever

The fears are forever, they never stop, they come with love. The fears of pregnancy evolve and do not disappear after delivery. The worries over the health of the child-to-be are replaced by fears over the Sudden Infant Death Syndrome, and later, leukemia, bad teachers and baby sitters, and risks of a stranger offering candy on the neighborhood streets. Parents worry about older children getting into a car with a friend who is driving and drinking. These fears are with us all the time with no end throughout our beloved children's lives. Anxiety and the wish to control, the resultant guilt, sadness, and anger are the inevitable consequences and burdens of taking on parenting. They will remain with us until our life is over. That is the cost of love.

The Loss of Joyful Anticipation

The desire for the perfectly healthy baby is commanding. If a problem during pregnancy has been a burden, hostile feelings may emerge toward the baby-to-be. Bleeding and the threat of miscarriage may cause a mother to wish for the miscarriage rather than have a defective child. If the pregnancy then continues, an awful mixture of feelings toward the baby-to-be may surface.

The wish to have the baby is mixed with angry, even murderous, feelings toward the growing fetus. Then there is the guilt, "How can I have such awful thoughts?"

Often, bed-rest is required for premature labor. Inevitable anger arises from being imprisoned in bed: "This child has taken over my body, I have no time nor space for myself. I can't do what I want. I now have to lie in bed for twenty-four hours of every day!" After the infant is born, resentment compounds this anger because the mother is again "incarcerated" by child care, particularly if she is nursing. A strong desire may arise in the mother to wean early this wonderful but intruding alien infant who has taken over her body and sense of self.

If a close friend or sister has had a miscarriage or delivered an infant with a serious problem, a pregnant mother may feel quite guilty about having and talking about her own healthy pregnancy.

Miscarriage

The ultimate loss of pregnancy. What can one say? There is no solace, only loss and sorrow, and no intellectualizing will take that away. It is only felt, painfully so, more often by the mother than the father. Such feelings as the failure to succeed in the rite of passage, the loss of a longed-for baby, and the fears about *ever* being successful and disappointing the excited relatives, all puddle into mourning.

Fortunately, almost all go on to have another. But that does not assuage the loss of the conceived child. And the worries of success do not go away until it is attained. No advice can take away these concerns. But the concepts in *Wish Versus Reality* below may be helpful, not in taking away the mourning but in the going on from there.

But something should be proffered that might "cut one's losses." Be careful in your exuberance, particularly if this is the second child or more. Explaining a miscarriage to a two-to-three-year-old sibling is not at all easy. In fact it is quite difficult. So it is best to inform them, and any relatives who might be truly disappointed, of the pregnancy *after* you have reached a stage where the outcome will result in a definitely viable infant. Babies in utero have a real chance of survival after twenty-eight to thirty weeks of pregnancy. So any time after that point is a better time to inform those who will be vulnerable to bad news.

15

Did he just kick you!?

CHAPTER II

Pregnancy and the Genesis of the Infant's Psyche

NURTURING THE PRE-BORN

The baby is not yet born. Yet he is a genetically preprogrammed machine. He will come into the world with the face, eyes, color of his hair, height, and temperament, among many other things, programmed from the genes that you, his parents, have given him. Almost all at this point is genetically preprogrammed.

Can he be influenced in utero? Yes, but only by physical things to the best of our current knowledge. Malnutrition, drug addiction, smoking, excessive alcohol, and certain viral infections can deleteriously affect the fetus. Fortunately most mothers are wise enough to get good prenatal care and avoid harmful substances. Additionally certain vaccines, such as that for German measles, have ameliorated the fear of viral damage to the fetus.

Nonetheless, some mothers worry: "I was really upset during my pregnancy, will that not affect him?" The answer to the best of today's knowledge is no, unless being upset leads to other problems such as drugs or excessive smoking.

IN UTERO STIMULATION

One musically inclined couple played, from a portable cassette recorder, a certain lullaby repeatedly on the mother's abdomen so that the infant would hear it. They swear that this same song is the best calming technique for their now born infant. As far as I know there is no substantive data regarding this. It is known that the human voice is calming to newborns. Perhaps that comes from hearing it in utero. But I am a firm believer in whatever works is great. Why not, if it causes no harm?!

IN UTERO ACTIVITY AND TEMPERAMENT

Many parents ponder if the activity of the unborn child is any indication of temperament. Again, to the best of my knowledge no research has shown activity in utero to be a reliable predictor. However, anecdotal experience reveals that often a baby who is highly active in utero may be born with a prowess for physical activity and, later on, athletics. Some babies are so active that they can literally tie their umbilical cords into knots. I have seen two infants born by c-section because they had created two overhand knots in their cords. I later on noted these infants to be quite agile and active as they grew up.

Every now and then a baby will be seen on sonogram to be sucking its thumb in utero. Such behavior, I believe, is one predictor of temperament. Almost always these infants will be born and display a "mellow," laid back, self-calming temperament which can be detected at birth and holds true throughout development. (See *Temperament* in Chapter VI)

17

What do you mean (calling me) Henrietta?

CHAPTER III

Pregnancy and the Reactions of Others

THE EXTENDED FAMILY

The extended family may set you up hoping you will fulfill their expectations.

Family Expectations, Part I

Mr. Sin related the following experience: "We originally for a long time thought we were not going to have any children. But somehow it happened. My family is Korean, and so far we don't have any boys as grandchildren for my parents. One of my brothers has a girl and another brother has three girls. All of our Korean friends were saying that my parents were sort of expecting a male grandchild. That was not my wife's and my expectation, but it was sort of rough on us because people around us would just put on that pressure." (story to be continued in chapter VII.)

Where does this pressure come from? Is it simply cultural? Do these parents have to feel the pressure of all previous generations?

Does this young pregnant couple of today have to go through this? Is it like pledging a fraternity? Do they have to suffer the same as all other couples in their family have? Are they expected to carry on the name of the family through the male child? And is having a girl here in America such a shame? Is this perpetuation of the concerns a part of the rite of passage for our particular culture? Perhaps all of the above? I leave it to you to decide.

"What do you mean, Henrietta?!"

The Erikson's were expecting. They had married late in their thirties and, feeling the biological time clock running out, decided to see if they could get pregnant as soon as possible, and it worked. The extended family was excited, as this was in fact the first grandchild since Mr. Erikson was the only child of his parents.

But the excitement escalated when amniocentesis revealed they were to have a girl! Mr. Erikson's mother Henrietta was a widow. She had longed for her son to have a child. She thrilled with the news of the pregnancy.

19

But, when she found out it was to be a girl she became elated beyond reason and pulled out all stops. She let it be known, through the relatives of course, that should her son decide to call this first and so far only grandchild Henrietta Erikson after herself she would right then and there take money from her own retirement fund and place it into an untouchable fund for her soon-to-be grand-daughter's total college education.

The parents-to-be, not having heard of this yet, had already decided to call their daughter Helen. They thought Helen Erikson sounded wonderful. The stage was set.

Aunt Britt, Henrietta's only sister, called one night and just let it drop that, "Oh, haven't you heard that your mother-in-law has promised that, should you decide to call your daughter Henrietta, this gift will be coming." Pregnant Mrs. Erikson was stunned. All she could get out of her mouth was, "What do you mean, Henrietta?!"

Fortunate for all Mr. and Mrs. Erikson showed restraint. They let it slide. Nothing was mentioned. Helen was born Helen; and Helen still received the gift.

This newborn has significance to more than just the parents. The coming of a newborn has importance, a rippling effect, throughout the extended family. It is as if this newborn belongs to more than just its parents! But that is not true.

The parents are the newborn's only parents. That is, in fact, the law. Sometimes, however, parents are forced to stand on their own two feet by defining just who is in control and to whom this infant belongs. They have to define themselves as the parents, and the coming infant as their child. That

is a critical part of the rite of passage. And any attempt to take away from them any aspect of their new parenthood is to diminish it. However, unconscious repetitive attempts exist in most cultures that are presented that can serve to make this rite of passage not so easy.

"OLD WIVES' TALES" BEGIN

Old wives' comments ("tales") are often warnings. If you do this or don't do that, this grave thing will happen. But think what power that gives to the one who is offering the warning: No matter what happens the one who warns wins. If you follow the advice, or warning, and everything works out, the one who warned you wins. If you don't follow the advice and things don't work out, it's because you did not follow the advice. "I told you so" is then the comment dreadfully anticipated by parents. If you ignore the warning and think things will work out all right, given the warning you received, you may live in fear of failure and be unable, out of worry, to enjoy success. Again, the one who warns wins; you must suffer just as he/she probably did when someone else tortured them with the same thing one generation ago.

Some comments seem almost meant to highlight the difficulties. They seem to say, "If I had to suffer, why should you have it any better?" Padded bras or larger lingerie may be given by a relative or the mother's mother with the fearful warning, "You'll need this because you'll have big leaky breasts in the hospital."

Other comments appear to make the commentator seem all-wise. Of course, that means you, the neophyte, might not be. "The baby is lying in your tummy in a way that I can just tell it's a girl." Others will say it's a boy by the way you look. All control appears theirs and none yours.

These intrusive comments made by local friends, neighbors, and relatives are more often than not resented by most mothers and fathers to be. "You're sooo big! Are you sure your doctor's right about the due date?" The mother knows she is sooo big, and can't wait until delivery reduces her.

It takes awhile for a first-time mother and father to feel confident and realize that these comments and feelings are the others' problems and not theirs.

THE BABY SHOWER RITUAL

More preparation bursts forth for this rite of passage. Toward the end of pregnancy, the women get together. Married and unmarried, with and without child, friends and relatives gather to celebrate, toward the end of pregnancy, the coming of the child. At the Bridal Shower items of intimacy are showered upon the soon-to-be bride. At the Baby Shower gifts are now rained upon the mother as aids for child care.

THE GRADING SYSTEM, THE BEGINNING OF COMPETITION

Parents become hard on themselves and start to expect perfection and control. An "A+" is perfection without any glitches. Glitches in the pregnancy begin to subtract from that grade. Others also become unconsciously involved in this grading process, as if it has always been this way. So it is as if they say to themselves: why not have the same old things dumped upon these new parents as have been dumped upon parents for generations. Most hardly ever step back and ask what are we saying and doing to these poor soon-to-be parents.

The Grading System

"It's true. People do grade you. Even in the Lamaze classes, you are graded on how well you breathe. Also, other pregnant mothers in the class come up to me and say, 'You mean you may have to have a c-section?! Aw, that's too bad!'"

"I am so worried that I won't breathe right…if I am even able to have a vaginal delivery. I am so worried that I'll scream. In my job and in my life, I am used to controlling a lot of things and situations. My greatest worry is that I'll be out of control. In fact, I'm terrified!"

The real accomplishment is not a grade on how you perform. The true "right" passage, is to manage as best as you can with the "hand that you are dealt." Almost all are respectful of that. However, let's be honest, parents compare and compete. And this is just the beginning of that. The above story also introduces the topic of "regression," or fear of it, and that will be dealt with in Chapter V.

21

"I could use a hug."

CHAPTER IV

Coping Concepts for Pregnancy

SURVIVING THE INTRUDER COMPLEX

Talk About It

Most often The Intruder Complex operates without our being aware of it. If we can recognize these feelings, we have a chance for mastering them. Otherwise, these feelings manipulate us and we lack control over them.

When feeling the jealousy and the loss of intimacy with one's spouse generated by The Intruder Complex, it is healthy to talk and simply share the feelings. Somehow or another merely sharing feelings relieves the ache. It hurts less if the other spouse hears it, listens, and just empathizes with your feelings. The spouse does not have to come up with some magical solution, he/she only needs to listen, hug, and be by your side.

Protect Your Life of Intimacy

Second, protect your life of intimacy by spending some time together. Sometimes, we fathers may feel we should be strong enough to handle all of this alone. We may believe it is a sign of weakness or a lack of adult maturity to say: "I need to talk with you." "I would like to spend some time together, with just you." "I could use a hug!" That is neither weakness nor flaw, that is wisdom. Those feelings are important and worth expressing. It takes maturity and courage to verbalize them.

Schedule time alone together to recover from all the efforts of preparation, telephone calls from relatives, and other consuming activities. If you can afford it, get an answering machine, or simply unplug the phone, and then sit on the porch together at the end of the day. That scheduled relaxing time together to repair is as important as any business appointment or required preparation for the baby to come.

To self-sacrifice yourselves to have a perfectly performed rite of passage is, most assuredly, unwise. To protect your life of intimacy together is not selfish, it is essential for an intact family. To protect the family, and that includes you as a couple, is one of the best things you can do for your coming baby.

Enhance the Paternal Instinct

For the mother the reality grows inside her. The father, while proud to have fathered, may be feeling the intrusion into the intimate relationship he has with his wife. His development of physical closeness with the infant comes only after delivery when he can hold this infant close to his chest and feel him snuggle warmly there. Imagine and daydream of this imminent feeling.

Also, there are other things a father can do to get close to this infant and beyond The Intruder Complex. Accompanying his wife to the obstetrician's office is protectively supporting her. Upon feeling his protective support, her warm thankful response back to him will enhance their closeness. Protectively sustaining his pregnant wife assuages the intrusion and still leaves the father with a sense of possession of not only the love for his wife but the budding love for his soon-to-be-born infant. Also, seeing the sonogram makes this infant visually real.

In the early months of this pregnancy, the growing protective-possessive instinct may be tenuous. Associated fragile fears may sporadically bubble up, especially when challenged by possessive controlling grandparents, but even with the pediatrician. One father quite openly and poignantly voiced them when choosing a pediatrician.

Finding a Baby Doc

A professional, mid-thirties couple came in for a private prenatal session just prior to the anticipated delivery. The father, posturing himself with his chin high and leaning back in his chair, challenged, "Tell me why I should use your practice."

I was astonished, but recovered and explained that perhaps the father could evaluate me, the pediatrician, during this prenatal session. I also expressed hoping to take advantage of this limited, valuable time for some education. With this apparently resolved, the session went forward. However, toward the end of the session, just after introducing The Intruder Complex, the father interrupted, "What I am looking for is a pediatrician who will enhance my fathering, and I don't think you're the one. I think I would be better off with a woman pediatrician. I had one as I grew up." "But more importantly," he declared with extraordinary candor, "I am not sure I want to see you developing a very close relationship with my wife and child."

Clearly, the father felt in tenuous possession of his wife and about-to-be-born infant. He was threatened, fearing that I was going to take his place. He was relieved to find out that I did not see myself as a threat to his fathering role. I explained that I hoped instead to develop a patient-physician relationship with the entire family and not just with his wife and child. I reconfirmed that I worked for them, the parents. They were "the boss." They were in control, and I was there simply to be of service to them and their child to the extent that they wished.

Interestingly, after delivery, the father held on so tightly to his new infant at each office visit, that I always had to perform the physical examination of their infant in the father's lap.

Should a father feel that way? Be sure to talk about it as this father did. At least discuss it with your spouse. Try to figure out where those feelings come from. The most likely reason is a ghost, a ghost from out of your own childhood that left you insecure, distrusting, and in tenuous possession of love.

Enhancers of Attachment

Attachment is the process of yearning for and delivering an infant with whom you develop a warm, intimate, trusting, and nurturing bond of love. However, you may be ambivalent about the pregnancy. Nonetheless the attachment is magnetic and the infant snags your heart. Thus, attachment is a process. It is not a fragile process, easily upset by some event or transient negative feeling.

The items below may be nice enhancers but they are not absolute essentials to the attachment process. Thus, if you are unable to attend a childbirth course or read a particular book, don't worry, the process of attachment marches on!

Preparation and Anticipation During Pregnancy The mutual involvement of parents, the team effort, in the preparation for the coming child may strengthen their intimacy together and decrease the uncomfortable lonely anxiety associated with doing anything for the first time. Childbirth education classes diminish angst. Sharing experiences with other parents-to-be is reassuring that the stress, changes, and feelings are common to all with a newborn regardless of their experience.

Less Anxiety and More Efficiency Knowledge decreases the anxiety of anticipating a new role and a new experience. Decreased anxiety makes for more enjoyable and successful parenting.

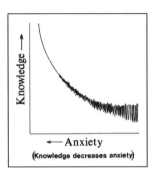

When these child and parent care concerns, from which this book was written, were assimilated into the course, the parents thoroughly enjoyed them. These parents felt that more knowledge decreased their anxiety, and less anxiety increased their efficiency. That left them with more time to relax and enjoy themselves and their infant.

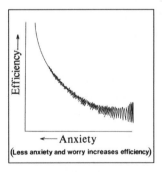

Fathers and mothers encouraged getting this information, this book, out to other parents, especially to those who, limited by time or money, are unable to explore all books on child care.

25

Child Birth Courses These courses are extremely helpful for learning what to anticipate. They dwell primarily upon how to deliver. They also go into what to expect in the hospital after delivery. They may also talk about infant nutrition.

Interview a Pediatrician Take this opportunity. See what he or she is like. Find out what the practice offers. Ask questions regarding child care after delivery. Find out about what he/she recommends regarding breast feeding and what is successful in that regard. Find out what books he/she suggests. Ask about common pediatric problems in the hospital such as jaundice. From this interview learn what to expect. Ask about home care issues such as dogs and cats, the pros and cons of visiting relatives, and safety issues such as what is the best position for sleeping to prevent Sudden Infant Death Syndrome.

Some pediatric groups offer courses on parenting. See what is available through them or local parents-after-childbirth groups. Often community organizations may offer child care courses.

Anticipate the Vortex of Birth Feelings Read ahead. Find out about regression and the early expressions of The Intruder Complex. Learn about the variations of newborn temperaments and compare that to your own, your spouse's, and the grandparents' expectations.

You even become a little harder to hug and hold onto.

HOW DO I PREPARE MY OLDER ONE FOR THIS UPCOMING CHILD?

William Penn...The Older Brother

William, now three years of age, had been a wonderful baby and child. Life could not have been better for the Penn family: everyone was healthy; Mr. Penn's job was going very well; and they had a beautiful house. Mrs. Penn had enjoyed staying home with William. She had a wonderfully close and happy relationship with him. She had breast fed him until he was eighteen months old after which he became very attached to his "bear-bear." He was allowed to stay up until around 11 P.M. every night to be with both parents. He enjoyed them so much it was hard to get him to sleep. They had delightful times together.

Mrs. Penn became pregnant. The first eight months were easy; the ninth was not. William refused to go to bed without a struggle. During the night he would wake up and come into his parents' room. It was an exasperating situation. Mrs. Penn spanked him for the first time and she felt absolutely terrible and guilty of failing as a mother. (story to be continued in the next book.)

While many, if not most, reading this chapter will be first-time mothers, some who are expecting will have already had a child. The inevitable question arises, how do I prepare my older one for the upcoming second child?

The Older Sibling

If the older sibling is beyond six or seven years of age, they will more than likely need little preparation. They may long for a younger sibling and want to hold him and show him to all their friends. And they somewhat have their own lives with friends and school, they do not feel the loss of the mother so much since they are preoccupied with their own schedules.

That is not so with the one-and-a-half-to-five-year-old child. They do not become jealous right away, they simply feel the loss of you, the mother. The older they are the more they think and anticipate this loss of you. And that shows up usually in the later part of pregnancy as acting out or reverting backwards such as the loss of toilet training — anything to get your attention. Parents cannot do something that will magically take away this problem, but there are some thoughtful actions that will soften the feeling of loss and cut the resultant expression of anger.

Photos of Them and You

Even if the older sibling is pre-verbal, put a photo of him in a frame on your bedside table. A strong silent message is given by that. It means he is in your thoughts, and he feels that. It is the same when you go to your own parents' house: it feels nice to see pictures of yourself around the house. Don't forget to take the bedside table photo to the hospital for delivery. When he comes to visit and sees himself sitting on the table

next to you even in the hospital, you won't have to say a word, he'll know you are thinking of him.

Also take photos of yourself and your husband and attach them to the mobile overhanging his crib. Or make a mobile with pictures hanging glued together back to back hanging from coat hangers safely out of his reach. If he is older, you can give him a wallet with pictures of yourself and your spouse in it for him to carry around.

Tape Your Voice

Another nice idea is to put your child in your lap and read to him from a picture book, or a story book with more or less pictures depending on his age. Capture the sound of your voice on an inexpensive cassette recorder (one company even sells a durable cassette tape recorder for children). Some people will have, or can borrow, a TV tape camcorder. You can use that also to capture the story book reading of yourself and your child. Then, when you are at the hospital away from this older child, or later on when home and unavailable (for example while breast feeding the new one), you can playback the recording of you and the older sibling for him to hear and see. You can also give him the book to look at while listening to or looking at the playback.

Create a Story Book

Another fun thing to do, if the older one is verbal, is to start your own story book. Take empty pages and once every day or so draw a cartoon story of what has, is, and will be happening. In other words, you can show yourself getting bigger and where the baby is, but you are still playing with the older

27

sibling. You can embellish the story, such as when you are going to the hospital you take a car, not a boat and not a plane. Draw these items and write the story underneath. Use simple crayons, and the drawings can simply be stick figures if you aren't good at art. Punch holes into the pages so you can tie them together into a growing book. But the final page should be one showing that, even though the baby is around and you are feeding him, you are still finding time to play and be with the older sibling.

Puppet Therapy

Puppet therapy, if the older one is verbal, can be fun and supportive. Your older child, if between almost two and five, is in the years of "magical thinking," where children have imaginary playmates and fanciful thinking. This magical thinking can be used in puppet therapy just before bedtime as a quiet and calm, but interesting, nightly ritual. Simply set up a family of puppets, or bears or other stuffed animals, that mimic your own situation. Thus a father bear exists along with a mother bear and a baby bear. And then the mother bear becomes pregnant. Then reenact, using the baby bear, some of the feelings you have noticed in your older child in response to your pregnancy or upsetting events of that day. You'll be shocked at what your older one will tell you about the feelings the baby bear has. These are his own feelings that he would hardly ever tell you directly. Then you can correct those feelings and reassure him that, for example if he is acting angry and upset, that the baby bear doesn't need to worry. His mother has a place in her heart that is just for him and no one else ever takes that place.

HOW DO I HANDLE THE OLDER ONE WHEN I AM CONFINED TO BED REST

Sometimes a mother of an older sibling will be forced into bed rest for many reasons to maintain her current pregnancy. How can she handle the acting-out older sibling who is feeling the loss of his bedridden mother? It is not easy.

First of all, remember the comments above regarding miscarriage and when to tell the older one. Use the cassette recorder and camcorder as outlined above during the times when you feel you need rest and a break from demands. But also set up a little step stool so that he can climb into your bed to be with you and read with you at times. That way you don't need to lean over and strain yourself by picking him up for a hug or to have him sit with you. You can, at your discretion, even eat together in bed this way.

Finally, we arrive at what I believe is the most important aspect of Coping Concepts for parents, and that is Wish Versus Reality.

WISH VERSUS REALITY

"Reality is a major source of stress...for those who are in touch with it." –Lily Tomlin, 1988

Wish Versus Reality conflicts occur if complications happen with pregnancy or delivery, even if the difficulty is a simple variation from normal. Parents-to-be dream of an uncomplicated pregnancy and delivery. Any reality less than that subtracts from the wishful dream and creates a conflict. To be told that a cesarean section must be anticipated can jolt parents out of their wishes for successful natural child birth and may thrust them into grieving. (See "The Emergency

Cesarean Section" and "A Lower Grade.") Early labor and being forced to anticipate a premature infant understandably create distress. Even the reality of an overdue baby can drive parents crazy as that confronts their wish to have the pregnancy over.

The discovery of a twin pregnancy may be a real challenge: A mother may be yearning to bond closely to a single child and, when told she will have twins, wonder how she can love two infants as much as one. Again, she wishes for and dreams of an uncomplicated bonding. But the reality of twins arriving engulfs her, and temporarily leaves her adrift with no control over what is happening. It is not what she had wished for. In fact, any complication of pregnancy (spotting, premature labor, or abnormalities with the sonogram or amniocentesis), will conflict with the wish for no glitches. The Grading System (see above) takes over.

What I have come to call Wish Versus Reality involves a concept of conflict, a conflict that arises frequently between what we really expect, or wish, to happen versus what actually happens. Understanding this conflict and its resolution serves us well in coping when reality confronts our everyday wishes for ourselves and our children to be.

Parents who have received most of their wishes throughout life are going to be the most vulnerable to the disappointments of reality. They may have been brought up protectively and constantly "rescued" from needing to solve their own disappointments and frustrations by their own overly solicitous parents. Others may also have been born with an inherent temperament of low tolerance

for frustration. Additionally, some parents may be in positions or professions where they are used to controlling situations. If we are parents in one of the situations described above, it is extraordinarily difficult to sometimes accept reality when it feels like it differs so much from what our wish was.

When in a Wish Versus Reality conflict, it is best to rationally look at what can be modified to meet your wishes. Sometimes one has to go into a damage-control mode in an attempt to cut your losses. But, if the reality is in the control of nature and not you or your spouse or the doctor, your best bet is to acknowledge that feeling of helplessness and come down to earth. We may wish we, or someone, had that kind of power — the power to fulfill every wish like a Genie — but the reality is that many situations are beyond the power of humans. While a truism, all our wishes do not always come true.

Share the feelings with your spouse. Talk about it. Even cry. But it is better to accept it. Better yet, anticipate inevitabilities. Other possible Wish Versus Reality conflicts are described above in "Losses & Fears." More on Wish Versus Reality will come throughout each chapter in this book.

And now onto/into the swirling vortex of delivery.

29

The Miraculous Rite

"HAVING A BABY IS A REAL SCREAM!"
JOAN RIVERS

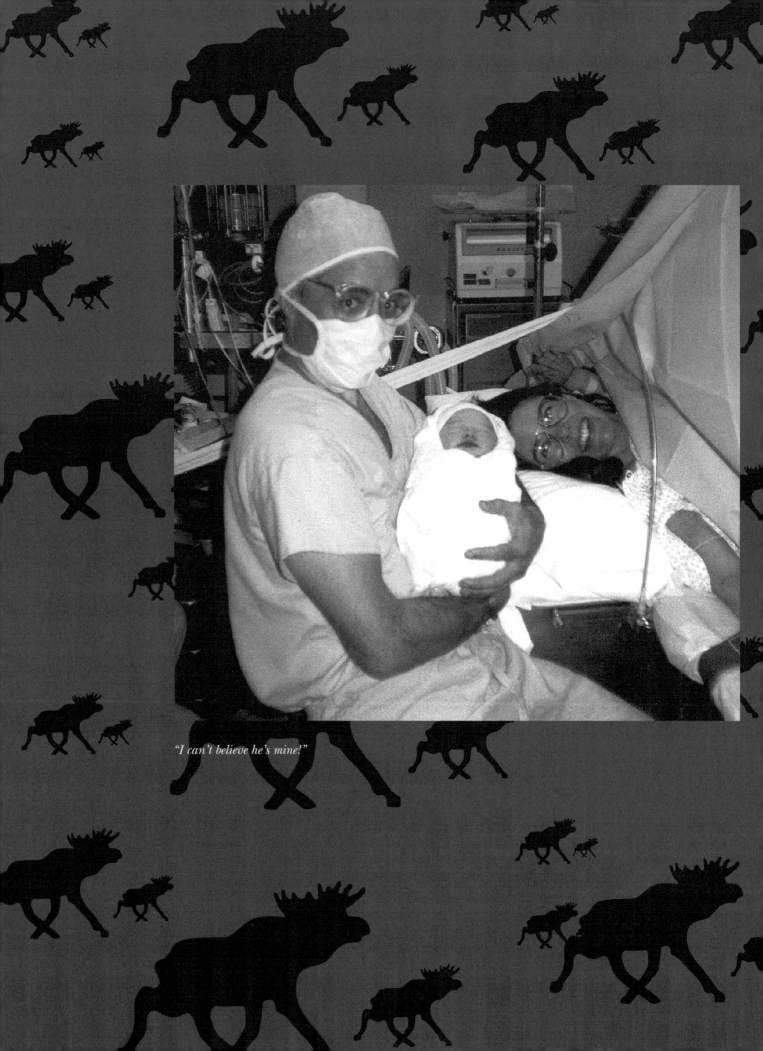

"I can't believe he's mine!"

Not Only Is a Baby Born But Parents Emerge

THE MIRACLE HAPPENS

"I can't believe he's mine!" –many parents

Suddenly out of the pain, the labor, the anguished worry, fatigue, and your distorted body comes this cry. A blue-to-pink head emerges followed by its slickly white-coated body. He is no longer an image on a sonogram. Cutting the cord ends the scurry of delivery. He is wrapped for warmth. His face wiped clean, you look into it holding him close to your body or on your chest and a wave of feeling engulfs you and all you can express in words is, "I can't believe he's mine!"

You have heard that no words can describe the feelings of seeing your baby born. It is true. It is a feeling, it is experienced…it is not at all easily captured in utterance. But of all phrases, the one that seems to forever recur, as you hold him for the first time, is, "I can't believe he's mine!"

Seeing the baby born never ceases to be absolutely wondrous. To behold another human coming from you (or your wife), and to observe him open his eyes and look out into a brand new world for the very first time is thrilling, exhilarating beyond description — miraculous! It quickly obliterates the memory of the painful, regressive, and uncontrolled experience of labor and delivery. Disbelief that this has happened to us, that the infant is truly ours, is felt by even the most starched of sophisticated parents.

Absolute awe is shudderingly interrupted by the anxious wait for reassurance of the baby's health. We listen for the first cry, and the word from the doctor or nurse regarding the baby's health and sex. And then, hopefully, we feel the thrill of relief that all is well.

THE LOSS OF INVINCIBILITY

Worry comes with love. No one can take it away. Love makes you vulnerable.

Rigid Old Boston

My wife was the third to have "rooming-in" at a Boston hospital. In those days the hospital refused "partial" rooming-in, thinking that, if the infant was in the mother's room and exposed to other adults as well as the mother, he could conceivably cause some infection upon return to the nursery. So my wife had "full" rooming-in and our daughter was in my wife's room day and night for the duration of the hospitalization.

I was the pediatrician on-call in the hospital the night of the delivery. After all had settled down from the delivery, I made rounds to look in on other patients. Later, about 2:00 a.m., I returned to my wife's room to peek in and see how she and our daughter were sleeping.

Upon entering, the shadow of my wife standing frozen and apprehensively watching our new daughter in the crib startled me. She turned toward me, fear on her face. Instantaneously feeling dread myself, I asked her, "What's the problem?" She quickly whispered, "I'm not sure she's breathing!" I looked at our daughter. She was quite pink, and breathing peacefully but quite quietly in a deep sleep after the exhaustion of delivery.

The first few days is often easy as one feels the ecstasy of having this wonderful infant. For most, exhilarating relief is felt when parents learn that the baby is healthy. Infrequently the early days may be difficult. Small, and sometimes large, medical problems may create anxiety — not only genuine conscious concern for the baby's health — but also unconscious worry about a glitch in our perfect delivery of a perfect baby. Most physicians are quite honest, reporting to you the problems along with perspective, such as whether it is a big or little problem, and what needs to be done. Fortunately, most difficulties nowadays are small and, even if large, are manageable.

The above vignette illustrates the universal fear of all us parents. We fear the responsibility about becoming the sole caretaker. Many mothers, feeling the instinctual need to be constantly observant and available, may often think that the father is of little help until after the first month of life. However, if a problem such as prematurity occurs, mothers report that the father is of real help and support from the start.

The overwhelming fear of feeling the need to be available all of the time again brings to the mother's consciousness that little time is left for herself. While great joy at being needed is savored, an unconscious resentment may emerge. On top of these concerns, one big worry often sits in the mind of parents, particularly the mother.

SO...WHAT KIND OF GRADE DID I GET?

We parents want to stand on our own two feet when delivering a baby. We seek to be in control and to perform well. In this rite of passage, we want a short, reasonable labor, preferably beginning on the due date, followed by an elegant delivery uncomplicated by glitches. So intensely do we wish for these, that actually we unconsciously grade ourselves in the process. Do you really grade this miracle of miracles?! Absolutely, we wish for perfection — a perfectly performed delivery producing a perfect baby.

Unfortunately There's No Elegant Way to Deliver a Baby!

Regression

Who's the Baby?

Mrs. Cobb had just delivered her first baby boy. It was very early in the morning when I went in to visit her. Her husband had left for home to get some rest. She had every reason to be ecstatic. She had no complications, and their baby boy was perfect and healthy. However, she was not happy at all. No matter what reassurance I offered, she continued to be depressed. I asked her what was the matter. She refused to answer. I asked her specifically about worries. She denied them all.

Just as I was reluctantly leaving, she blurted out, "I acted like such a baby! I screamed and yelled all during the delivery. They must have thought I was such a baby!"

Ten Years Later

Another mother whose children were in their preteens echoed the persistence of that feeling, "Even now, ten years later, I get a knot in my stomach every time I drive by that hospital and look up to the third floor [which is where the labor and delivery suites are]!"

Macho Men

Even macho fathers have embarrassingly exclaimed the exact same words, "I acted like such a baby!" because they felt shame about crying with joy when seeing their own infant born.

There is no elegant way to deliver a baby! Delivery is a perfectly natural time to lose control. It is a time when parents usually and very understandably regress. As Joan Rivers the comedian quipped, "Having a baby is a real scream!" Fortunately, in the past ten years, labor and delivery room personnel have been trained to be more empathetic with the difficulties and feelings of delivering parents.

If anyone has a problem with your crying out, moaning, or tears, it is their problem, not yours! To fear the pain of labor and feel embarrassed about crying out is normal. Sometimes with delivery you even pass stool, which is humiliating with an audience, even for the least modest of mothers. It is understandable to dislike the thought of others seeing every bit of you, and what you might feel is a regressive experience.

Regression confronts the wish for a sense of real self achievement. It is often perceived not only as a loss of self-control but also a loss of identity and self-confidence, not to mention dignity.

Vaginal Delivery The delivery of our own child by someone else, namely the obstetrician, threatens our protective-possessive instincts. Aware of these feelings, many obstetricians now involve the father in the vaginal delivery. Recently, a father told me of the exhilaration he and his wife felt at having the delivery turned over to them. After the shoulders and head had been delivered by the physician, the father delivered the rest of his infant's body. He even cut and tied the umbilical cord!

We parents dislike the feeling of not being in control. It is a regressive feeling, causing fear about being younger, or childlike, at a time when we have put a lot of effort into maturing and taking on new roles. Regression often also recalls, by highlighting in our conscious mind, our own fears and tenuous acceptance of going forward with these new roles.

C-sections

For Fathers

The Emergency Cesarean Section

Both parents attended the childbirth course and were prepared, very excited, and anxiously anticipating the delivery. They had familiarized themselves with labor and delivery techniques. They felt in control and aspired to manage the delivery pretty much on their own. Labor began. All was progressing as anticipated.

Suddenly, the fetal monitor showed severe, prolonged decreases in the fetal heart rate indicating the unborn baby was in distress. The obstetrician recommended, and quickly performed, the needed emergency Cesarean section.

Their baby was delivered. He had a true knot in his short cord. With every contraction as he progressed down the birth canal, the knot became tighter and tighter cutting off his circulation. His life and mental development were saved by the emergency Cesarean section, performed so promptly and properly.

The father stayed with his wife during the operation. He went home late that night and, while taking a shower before going to bed, began to sob and sob — all alone.

He later described his feelings: "I never felt so helpless in my entire life. I was expecting to be in control and to help her through delivery. And yet, someone else, the obstetrician, had to take over to save my baby. I could only stand there, helpless and worried. I had to trust this man with the lives of the two most important people in my life, my wife and child. I was with my wife for only a few visits to the obstetrician before this delivery. I had only just met this obstetrician a few months ago, and had spent mere moments with him during my wife's visits."

As the complications of delivery have decreased, there has been an increase in the number of Cesarian sections over the past decade. A recent article noted that nation-wide the incidence of Cesarian sections was 24%, and that in the Washington, D.C., metropolitan area, the rate of Cesarian sections was 28% of deliveries. Translated, that means that any pregnant mother stands a one-in-three to one-in-four chance of a Cesarian section. For parents who have worked hard together to learn how to breathe and manage their own labor and vaginal delivery, it is discouraging to have that training suddenly go to naught.

I have felt that impotent exclusion, as described above in The Emergency Cesarian section, with my first child's birth (See The Brass Bars). It was not simply the feeling of being separated, but rather it was the help-less loss of my wife and child-to-be, and the sense of not being able to protect or con-trol anything, especially at a time when I wanted to stand on my own two feet. It was in someone else's hands, not mine.

At the time of delivery, we fathers often feel excluded. We resent our lack of com-mand and our often forced, reluctant, helpless abrogation of this control to the obstetrician. We can feel silently angry and testy. We can, sometimes, cover up our fears by being overly solicitous in hopes of manipu-lating for better, more individualized care. It is not at all easy for us to pass over the care and survival of the two most important people in our lives, our wife and new child, to an obstetrician whom we have hardly known.

WELL? I KNOW MY DELIVERY WAS NOT AN A, USING DRUGS AND ALL. BUT HOW DID I DO? B? B-? C?

For Mothers

A Lower Grade

One mother who required an emergency Cesarian section had a very healthy infant. I came again to visit her on the fifth day after birth just as she was preparing to go home. Her infant was quite healthy, but he had developed the nuisance problem of breast milk jaundice. I told her her infant was fine, but this minor annoyance would have to be further managed over the next three to four days. She bemoaned, "Oh, no! First I had to have a Cesarian section, and now there is this breast milk jaundice! Nothing is going right!"

Everything was going right in terms of this mother and her infant's health. But, in terms of her success at delivering and feeding her child on her own, it was as if she had received a "B" instead of an "A".

Delivering an infant is a rite of passage. All parents wish for no complications, difficulties, or setbacks in becoming independently grown-up. The wish is to perform child birth perfectly, with no glitches. Because of the importance to perform and perform well, parents unfortunately grade themselves and others.

THE HOSPITAL: A SECURE PLACE?

After delivery a mother is, most often, thrilled with accomplishment. She sleeps soundly and without fear, knowing enough people are around observing the baby. Whether the delivery is at home, a birthing center, or in the hospital with or without "early discharge," most mothers prefer a setting where they can rest comfortably in the knowledge that someone competent, other than themselves, is with the baby.

Self grading, however, always exists and parents often are quite tough on themselves. This self-censorship can be made more or less worse — or better — by the scrutinizing eyes of the hospital personnel.

As the time to leave nears, a parent may fear relinquishing the security of the hospital. "At home, everything depends on me. Will I be able to handle it? I'm worried." This is the fear of being successful when all alone and everything depends on you.

Other parents may want to leave as soon as possible — some to avoid the costs. Others may fear a loss of control over their new baby, thinking that the knowledgeable hospital staff will take over. Others may not like adjusting to hospital rules, such as those involving visitors. Some may not relish the ambience of the hospital, feeling it is a place of illness and death. Some may simply feel they cannot get any rest there. Also a distrust for hospitals and doctors is enhanced if a parent had a previous bad experience with a physician or hospital.

The Brass Bars

Twenty-five years ago, our daughter was born in the best of Boston's obstetric hospitals. As the father, I was not allowed in the delivery room. Yet, being the pediatrician-on-call in the hospital that night, I would have had to dash in and handle any newborn problem, even though it was my own daughter being born. I was, however, allowed to be with my wife during labor.

As the time for delivery approached, my wife was wheeled away in her hospital bed to the elevator taking her to the delivery room one floor below. The elevator was old-fashion with vertical brass bars, polished in their middles by years of constant handling. The bars pulled across the opening as a ceiling-to-floor safety barrier.

I was allowed to go as far as this elevator. My wife was wheeled onto it, and the brass bars came across separating her from me. The vision of her descending out of sight during her pangs of labor is indelibly seared into my memory. All I could do was helplessly watch as I gripped the bars anxiously.

Initially a test of confidence.

Many hospitals are responding to these feelings. Fathers now are invited into the delivery. Birthing rooms look more like home. The mother's room is often decorated, sometimes even luxuriously. Certain hospitals allow relatives or extremely close friends to be present at delivery, along with the father, if the parents request it. Fathers are frequently allowed to stay overnight in the same room. Visitations by older siblings are now commonly permitted.

Parents now are no longer mutely awed by their doctors. They feel secure enough to explain their feelings to the obstetrician or pediatrician. Their physician can then understand and respond to their desire to leave the hospital early, or to remain, for a little bit, feeling the safety of the hospital setting.

BREAST FEELINGS: INITIALLY A TEST OF CONFIDENCE

Proving Something?
"Everyone wants me to breast feed. But I'm not sure I'll be successful. I don't know. Maybe I'll try it and see if it works. I know it's supposed to be better for the baby. But, at my age, I'm not into trying to prove something. Actually, I think I'd prefer formula."

Tension is sensed by all of us when doing anything for the first time. We feel insecure, some of us more so than others. Many mothers may feel confident in the hospital, but upon arrival home become anxious.

"All of this depends on me. No one else can breast-feed this child. I don't know if I can do it. What if it doesn't work?" These discomforting feelings, if excessive, can interfere with breast-feeding.

While many truly enjoy breast-feeding, others are conflicted. While breast-feeding is recommended, many obviously opt for formula. Others will do both.

UNABLE TO BE HAPPY ABOUT SUCCESS?

This may sound strange, but the initial tentative ecstatic feelings of becoming a parent can be compounded by fears and, indeed, guilt about actually being successful. Fears and guilt often erupt from within us when our wish to stand alone on our own two feet as new parents confronts the necessity to give up needing our own parents in the process of becoming successful parents ourselves. Some of us, in becoming parents ourselves, may feel we are losing the dependent relationship with our own parents; and we may not want that. Thus we fear being successful in our new role and can become depressed, sometimes seriously so, because we may lose our old role as a dependent son or daughter. We may feel alone. While new parents' relationships with their own parents are the most common cause for new parents to feel guilty about success, interactions with others may cause the same problem.

One mother's older sister had tragically died in the fifth month of pregnancy from a brain tumor. This mother felt terrible about being happy she had a healthy new baby boy and that things were going so well for her own family. Another mother confided, just hours after the delivery of her own very healthy, big, baby boy, "I told my husband that I feel like wrapping up this beautiful new baby of mine in a blanket and giving him as a gift to my sister." Her sister had a very premature newborn who developed multiple severe complications resulting in permanent lung and brain injury. This mother expressed an obsessive guilt because her child was so healthy.

We feel vulnerable when these things happen to people who are close to us because it could happen to us. And, when it does not, then we are happy that we are free from the problems. They have not happened to us. If it has to happen at all, let it happen to someone else. But that last perfectly normal and understandable thought, which bubbles up from the cauldron of the unconscious into our daylight mind, causes any sensitive person to feel guilty and then depressed, sometimes to the point of being immobilized. That kind of guilt can freeze a parent and subsequently stymie successful fathering, mothering, or nursing.

But that thought, the thought alone, did not cause the medical problems. Nobody's thoughts are that powerful. The thought alone is harmless and normal, although usually kept to oneself.

FATHERS

Become Ensnared From the Start

Fathers sometimes can, unfortunately, be a bit "workaholic" and/or feel overburdened, or indeed bothered by a newborn. However, if we become involved during the pregnancy, delivery, and early child care, we may just become irresistibly ensnared by this wonderful new product of our efforts.

And Kamikaze From the Start

Even just after delivery many fathers will toss, or hold, their small newborns into the air much higher than what mothers are ever comfortable with. In a later book you will read more about the Kamikaze Mode which describes the father's adventuresome attachment with his child (For now, see the Glossary).

PINKS AND BLUES

Aside from dressing them differently, do we treat girls differently from boys even in the newborn period? The answer is yes. A study showed that we parents are quicker to console a crying baby girl and are, in comparison, slower to pick up a crying baby boy. It was as if the parents unconsciously expected that boys should be able to handle whatever was bothering them while girls needed more protection and/or gentler handling.

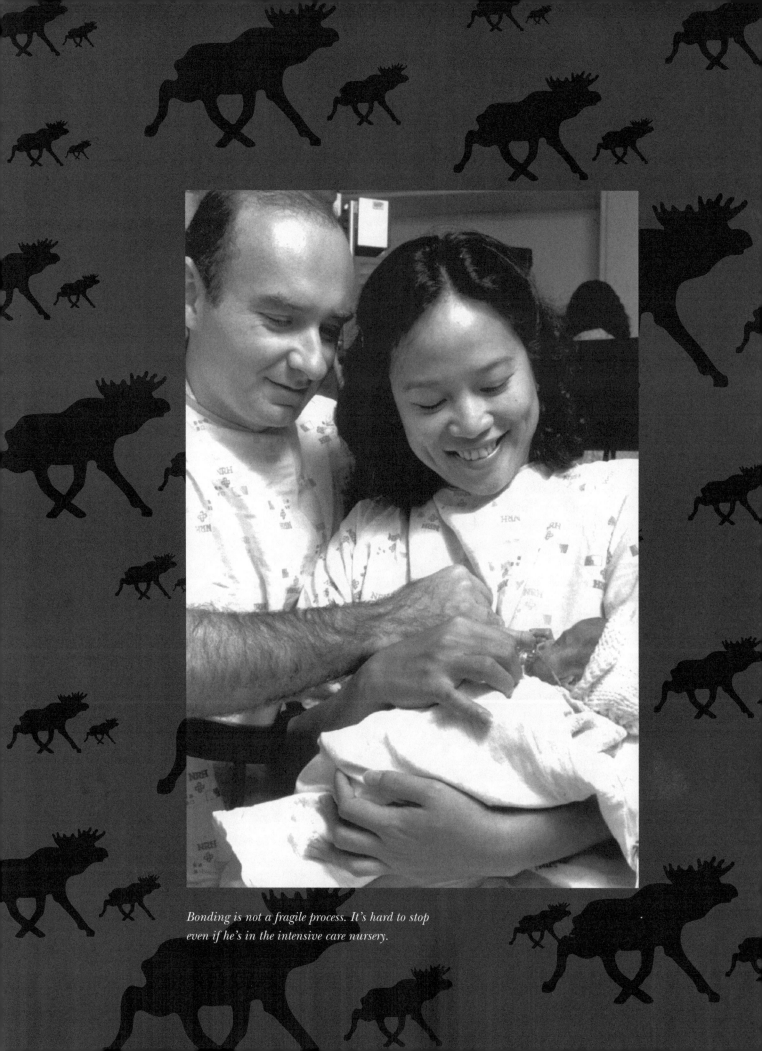

Bonding is not a fragile process. It's hard to stop
even if he's in the intensive care nursery.

The Genesis of the Newborn's Psyche

WHAT IS BONDING AND ATTACHMENT?

It Is a Process, Not an Event

Many parents still hear that, if they are unable to hold or breast feed their infant immediately after delivery, then bonding may not be as strong as it could be. This is untrue. Many times a mother or an infant has either a minor or major complication after delivery, and treatment may require that they miss each other right after delivery. And yet they still bond. In fact, surviving a difficult experience together can even enhance an attachment. Bonding is a process; it is not a single event which, if missed, could cause irreparable damage.

It Is Not a Fragile Process

Attachment is not fragile. An enormously strong process evolves which can withstand vehement pressures. It is capable of surviving the most difficult, challenging circumstances. Even children who are adopted will attach firmly and lovingly to the adopting parents.

Parents and infant bond even when enhancers of bonding are temporarily lost and obstacles great. While anticipation and desire for an infant are helpful, parents bond to a child from an unexpected, sometimes even unwanted, pregnancy. While breast-feeding enhances closeness, particularly when initiated immediately after delivery, parents also attach to infants suddenly taken to intensive care nurseries. Parents attach to formula-fed infants and tube-fed premature babies in incubators.

While pregnancy and the early months of life are very important periods, bonding progresses over the lifetime of the child and parents. The process of attachment is enhanced by many events, approaches, and behaviors. None of them are absolutely critical, and only severe psychological or physical cataclysms block bonding.

WHAT IS A NEWBORN LIKE?

Is He Just Needs and Reflexes?

The newborn, while tired after delivery, often quickly awakens to look into this new world of his. His needs and reflexes then become apparent. How they are expressed and how he controls them is modulated by his temperament.

His needs are hunger, warmth, and closeness. The most obvious reflexes are the rooting, sucking, startle, and grasp reflexes. Initially anyone can care for him. He is dependent on others for his survival. He may demand and cry to have his needs met while often giving little in return other than to absorb snuggling with you. He is not socially responsive other than complaint whimpers, cries, or screams. But he is capable of interaction; he does recognize that something has been done in response to his demands. And he communicates with his cry, often as if talking while crying.

Temperament: The Great Modulator

The Ends of the Spectrum An individual newborn's temperament, or for that matter a child's or an adult's, modulates the levels at which he senses incoming stimuli and the levels of his outgoing expressions and activity. Some newborns startle and scream when their diaper or clothes are changed while others are not at all bothered by this. Cold hands, or even a warm bath, may be highly irritating to some infants and not to

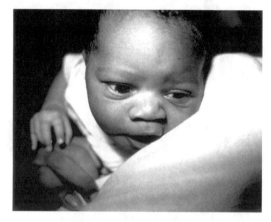

The Rooting Reflex: As his cheek touches your arm his mouth turns toward it rooting for a nipple.

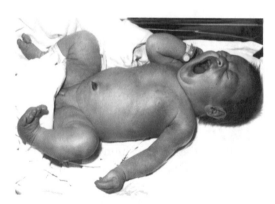

A mellow yawn? Yes...note the one arm down and the other up much like a teenager who has been woken up.

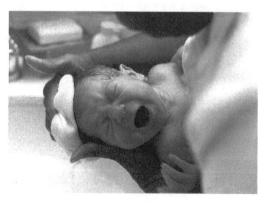

For the truly high-strung newborn, even a warm bath will evoke screaming frustration.

others. Certain infants will scream while others only softly complain.

I think the easiest way to look at newborn temperament is to view it as a spectrum with the "mellow, laid back" infant at one end and the "high-strung" newborn at the other end. In the newborn period, some infants have more control over the newborn reflexes than others. These newborns are able to move their extremities more smoothly, even to the extent of being able to intentionally suck on their hand or thumb just after birth. These infants we describe as having the "mellow, laid back" type temperament. Sometimes just after birth, especially with an infant with the "mellow, laid back" type of temperament, the beginnings of social responsiveness can be seen and felt when eye contact is obtained. This newborn can be consoled with a soft understanding voice. Rarely, in the immediate newborn period, he may actually smile in response to endearing sounds. More often though, the mellow newborn is rewarding to his parents with his contentment and cuddliness. The mellow newborn is able to already calm himself without your help.

Infants at the other end of the spectrum of disposition have little control over their newborn reflexes. And this infuriates them, particularly if they have a low tolerance for frustration as a part of their temperament. These "high-strung" newborns are hypersensitive, hyper-reflexive, frustration-intolerant, and unable to calm themselves. They have the disconcerting task, during the early weeks, of mastering control of their reflexes in order to learn to calm themselves down. Only then can they go on to purposeful movements like sucking their thumb and smiling, and soon after that cooing.

The ability to be consoled is also dependent upon individual temperament. The mellow infant is much more easily consoled than the infant with the high-strung disposition, but both are consolable. The high-strung infant simply requires more calming techniques, as described below in Chapter Eight.

Our Fears and Our Longed-for Images
During pregnancy it is usual for parents to have fears, especially about the baby's well-being. These fears, while often conscious, can also appear as frightening dreams. However, in addition to the fearful images, parents begin to form positive thoughts of the baby-to-come. We often daydream about what it will be like to hold and cuddle our baby, whether it will be a boy or a girl, and how the baby will respond when we talk to him. There is a wishful, warm yearning for the baby. Then the baby is born and our thoughts and longings are abruptly confirmed or denied — by the baby and his temperament.

45

*A mellow baby in conflict: The self-calming suck
loses to the irritating grasp reflex.*

The "Mellow, Laid Back" Infant The
"mellow" newborn is what most parents are
dreaming of. He is calm, laid-back, quiet,
and easily snuggles into the nap of your
neck. He cuddles. He melts into your body.
When awakened from a sound sleep he,
like a teenager, will yawn stretching one
arm up and the other down while arching
his back. *(See photos on page 44)* He is able to
move his arms smoothly through the air, so
steadily that he succeeds in getting his hand
to his mouth. He is capable of calming himself by simply sucking his fingers or thumb.
This cuddler's hands are often seen in the
open position as his arms move through the
air. Or, they are clenched as he tucks them
under his chin to prevent them from flying
out in a startle reflex.

Most parents of a cuddler wonder if he
can even hear. One mother was panicked
that her baby couldn't hear. She worried
aloud, "I dropped a garbage can next to
his crib and he did not even budge." Loud
noises or parents' cold hands do not bother
the mellow newborn.

When he cries, it is more often a gentle
complaining soft whimper curling his lower
lip down with more pout than fury. He
modulates his cry, meaning that a little irritation causes a little cry, moderate irritation
a moderate volume of crying, a lot of irritation and a loud cry. But even with a lot of
irritation, he often won't even cry at all.

It takes a lot of stress to startle him. You
almost have to pinch him or toss him into
the air so he feels himself falling to elicit
even the slightest startle reaction. When he
does startle, his arms extend out, but he
quickly aborts the reflex and pulls them

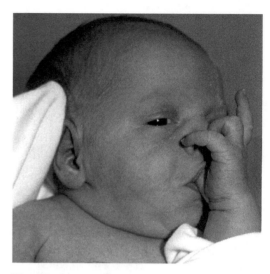

The self-calming suck begins.

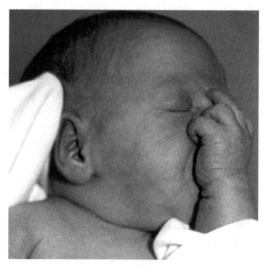

*But then the uncontrollable and irritating grasp reflex
gouges into his lip, nose, even the roof of his mouth.*

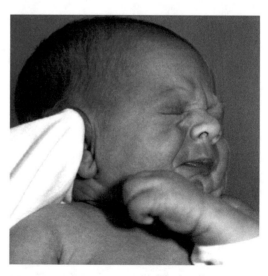

*He grimaces but does not scream and go into an
out-of-control startle reflex.*

46

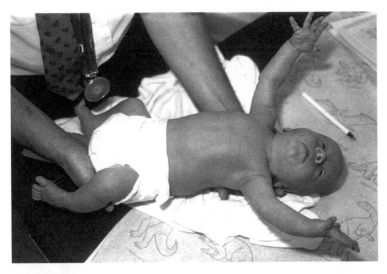

The aborted startle reflex of a "mellow" newborn.

The startle starts.

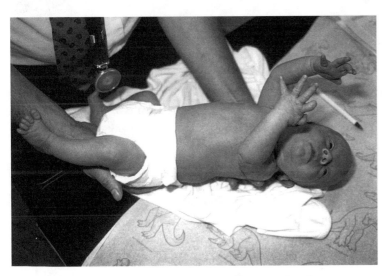

But no cry! He begins to abort it and pulls his arms close to his chest.

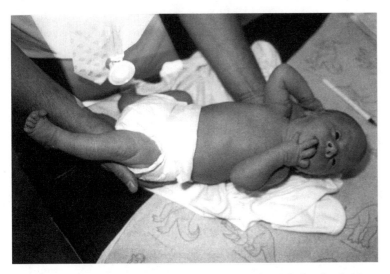

He pulls his hands down stabilizing himself by using his right hand to hold onto the caretaker's supporting hand while his left hand enters his mouth.

The high-strung newborn even when swaddled will sometimes intensely complain, but it is usually less than when not swaddled.

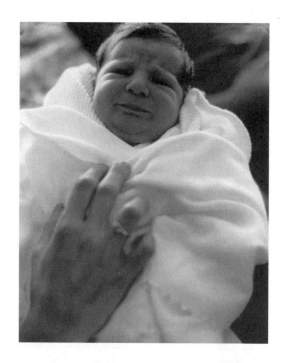

back, holding them closely to his chest under his chin. He is tolerant of changes in his environment. The hallmark of a mellow newborn is that he is not easily upset and, if upset, he has the ability to quickly calm himself.

The "High-strung" Newborn One mother exclaimed, "He never acted like a baby!"

This type of temperament (for an example, see The Carefree Socialite in Book II to follow) has had several labels, all of which describe different aspects of the disposition. Dr. Spock called him "hypertonic." Twenty years ago this kind of newborn was dubbed the "jittery newborn." One of the latest titles is hypersensitive. But these infants are often not just hypersensitive, they are hyper-reflexive and frustration-intolerant. More-over, they express their intolerance. They are "intense!" That is the most commonly used word of parents when they are describing their baby. Even when swaddled they will at times complain. Sometimes these newborns are, as first noted by Dr. Brazelton, smaller than expected for the length of the pregnancy.

High-strung newborns are completely dominated by the newborn reflexes, parti-cularly the startle and grasp reflexes. When you wake them from sleep and roll them over onto their backs, even ever so gently, they are hypersensitive to your cold hands and the change of position with rolling. They startle with their arms stiffly flying way out and around with their hands open and fingers stiff. This motion is followed by the arms and hands coming back toward the head rather than the chest. The grasp reflex takes over as the fingers touch their heads. If they touch their cheeks, mouth, ears, or hair, they cannot stop themselves from painfully grabbing, scratching, and pulling.

They may then stiffly arch their backs. If on a flat firm surface, like that of a changing table or even the firm crib mattress, they rock because only the backs of their heads and feet are touching the surface. When you look at their faces, panic is present. They lose their breath for a slight moment and clearly look as if they fear they are falling. They then scream with obvious frustration and rage and appear furiously intolerant of this lack of control over these reflexes. This screaming and startling rapidly and constantly repeat in a vicious vortex of lost control.

Unlike the mellow newborn, the "high-strung" kid is unable to move his arms smoothly. He may try to put his hand to his mouth, but he becomes furious as the grasp reflex pulls at his lips. Also, these jerky movements may interfere with successfully getting his hand into his mouth. His frus-trated frown is followed by a high-pitched, angry scream which goes right through your heart. And then his startle reflex is relent-lessly renewed. He feels jerked around and he is smart enough to resent it. In fact, he is furious over this loss of control.

The high-strung newborn is overly reactive to any sensory stimuli. The slightest sound or the most minuscule touch will, more often than not, evoke the furiously frustrating startle reflex. The parents have no doubt that their infant is able to hear. Simply closing a door can set off the screaming startle reflex.

These babies are also intolerant of frustration. Lack of control over the newborn reflexes drives them and their parents crazy. They are exasperated with their inability to calm themselves. They express this frustration very frequently, loudly, and quite intensely.

Also, infants with this temperament appear to have no "volume control," like that on the radio or TV. They simply have an "on-off" switch. Either they are wonderfully fine or they are madly screaming. A small irritating stimulus, such as simply trying to lift his own head, will flip the switch and a great deal of intense exasperation will be expressed by screaming. The mellow baby on the other hand, responds with just a little complaint cry or whimper if the displeasure is only minor. The cry of the mellow, laid-back newborn is modulated.

The Spectrum of Temperament Many variations exist in the spectrum between the "mellow" and the "high-strung" newborn. Some babies have a very strong temper and clearly display a will of their own. They have a very angry cry and arch back, as opposed to the gentle complaint cry of the mellow infant. It is as if they are "sticking up" for themselves. But they may also be able to calm themselves down. They may not be dominated by the newborn reflexes which irritate the completely "high-strung" newborn. Others may be uncommonly and precociously independent even from birth.

While some would like to simplify temperament, including myself, it is quite complicated and must have multiple genetic determinants. An understanding of tempera-

ment must include: newborn reflex control, sensitivity to external stimuli, pain threshold, frustration tolerance, adaptability, activity level, intensity of reactions, attentiveness and curiosity, and later on fearfulness, and interaction with others (are they outgoing and self-confident or shy?).

Can Parents Determine a Newborn's Temperament? While studies are mixed, I and others believe that certain characteristics of temperament are apparent from birth. Parents sense it within minutes of handling their own newborn. It can be assessed by simply observing him, for example, during feeding or changing clothes. Watch as you roll him over and wake him from a sound sleep to change his diaper. Observe as you take off his clothes and pull his arms out of the sleeves. Watch him and look at the following (albeit non-scientific but quite reasonable) TENP Scale which will quickly and easily help you figure out your baby's disposition. And then see if those aspects of his temperament don't stay with him for the rest of his life!

The spectrum of temperament: Some babies have a temper but are able to calm themselves. Notice the intense anger but no startle reflex. This examination was not what he had in mind.

49

TEMPERAMENT EVALUATION OF THE NEWBORN (TENP) SCALE

Initial instructions for the TENP Scale

Read each item of the Scale. Choose and mark the letter of a particular item that best describes your infant. If an item has not been observed (for example reactions to bright lights), then skip that item.

■■

1 REACTION TO LOUD NOISES
❏ A) has no response and you're worried that he can't hear
❏ B) squirms with slight aborted startle reflex
❏ C) blinks and goes into a total startle reflex with scream

2 AMOUNT AND INTENSITY OF CRY
❏ A) cries mainly when hungry, curls lip down, and is consolable
❏ B) screams a lot, often with a shrill, and then is hard to console
❏ C) cries hardly ever

3 THUMB SUCKING
❏ A) fails attempts to do so, becomes furious with a shrill scream along with repetitive startle reflexes
❏ B) sucks thumb or hand at will
❏ C) tries to get it in and eventually prevails but with some frustration

4 WHILE AWAKE THE BABY
❏ A) acts fussy and frustrated with screaming startle reflexes when on back; becomes furious with frustration at being stuck when on abdomen
❏ B) behaves quietly and snugly
❏ C) whines with frustration when placed on abdomen, but is otherwise active and alert

5 REACTION TO BRIGHT LIGHT
(for example a camera flash)
❏ A) has no response, possibly a blink
❏ B) blinks, then squirms irritated, and/or whines
❏ C) blinks with a quick, total startle reflex and shrill cry

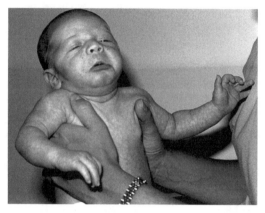

Notice the curled down lower lip associated with the modulated cry of the laid-back mellow newborn's complaints.

6 MODULATION OF CRY
❏ A) cries with an on-off switch; the cry turns on in a flash and then turns off just as quickly; the cry is furious, often out-of-control, frustrated, and high in pitch
❏ B) begins to whimper and sputter, builds up and comes down slowly (like a volume control on a radio); the cry is more often mild to moderate and not a high-pitched scream; may hardly ever cry

7 WHEN PLACED ON BACK, THE BABY
❏ A) attempts to use one or both elbows to hold himself stable and occasionally startles and complains
❏ B) thinks he is falling, rocks frantically out of control with repetitive startle reflexes and shrill scream alternating with silent stunned fright when he thinks he is falling. Grasp reflex catches hair and face
❏ C) lies calmly, able to place both elbows to the side as stabilizers to keep himself from feeling as if falling (see page 67, photo C)

8 SLEEPING
- ❏ A) requires some effort to be put to sleep; usually sleeps the same amount of time as awake time
- ❏ B) goes to sleep easily and sleeps 16-18 hours per day
- ❏ C) fights going to sleep, sleeps around 6-8 hours per day, and is very colicky in evenings

9 REACTION TO COLD HANDS OR COLD STETHOSCOPE
- ❏ A) responds with a total startle reflex often accompanied by a loud angry shrill scream
- ❏ B) squirms, makes an irritated grimace or cries
- ❏ C) has no response but for possibly a slight squirm

10 THE STARTLE REFLEX
- ❏ A) startles hardly ever and if so it is aborted with pulling hands close to the chest
- ❏ B) startles but settles with your help (e.g. if you hold his hands to his chest, if you place his elbows against the table or if you let him suck on your finger or a pacifier)
- ❏ C) screams madly with a total frightened startle reflex with arms out and around and is very hard to soothe

11 WHEN GIVEN A BATH THE BABY
- ❏ A) screams angrily and continues with every stroke of the wash cloth (see page 44, bottom photo)
- ❏ B) becomes initially upset but adapts with occasional cry
- ❏ C) enjoys it, finds it fun

12 WHEN CHANGING CLOTHES OR DIAPER
- ❏ A) complains to some extent with whimpering or aborted startling
- ❏ B) doesn't mind it at all
- ❏ C) startles, screams and doesn't stop angry crying until changing is completed

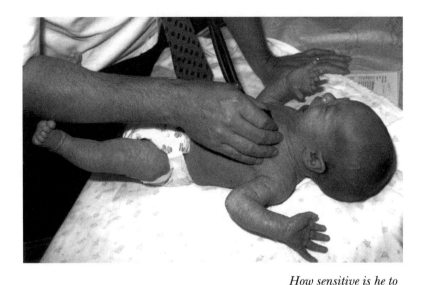

How sensitive is he to touch and the discomfort of cold hands and a cold stethoscope.

13 SOOTHING
- ❏ A) soothes with some amount of effort on your part, but eventually sputters down to calmness
- ❏ B) soothes only with extreme efforts on your part often requiring one calming technique attempt after another. In fact he is often inconsolable
- ❏ C) needs hardly any soothing; if soothed, it is quickly effective

14 IF BREAST-FEEDING
- ❏ A) has difficulty in initiating breast-feeding, frantically thrashes, is unable to latch on, screams furiously with frustration, tosses head and body back, and takes bottle nipple more easily than breast nipple
- ❏ B) shows no frustration and immediately latches onto nipple
- ❏ C) demonstrates some frustration with infrequent complaint crying, but then takes either breast or bottle nipple

15 REACTION TO PAIN (e.g. blood test)
- ❏ A) cries slightly with some complaint, a wiggle withdrawal movement, and perhaps an aborted startle reflex
- ❏ B) hardly responds to pain unless it is intense, may show some slight wiggle withdrawal movements
- ❏ C) immediately pulls away with a total startle reflex and loud angry shrill cry

51

SCORING INSTRUCTIONS

Now that you have completed the questionnaire, look at the SCORING KEY.

For each item, find the number that corresponds to the letter and record the number in the score box.

SCORING KEY:

Question #	Scoring Box	A	B	C
1	☐	1	2	3
2	☐	2	3	1
3	☐	3	1	2
4	☐	3	1	2
5	☐	1	2	3
6	☐	3	1	2
7	☐	2	3	1
8	☐	2	1	3
9	☐	3	2	1
10	☐	1	2	3
11	☐	3	2	1
12	☐	2	1	3
13	☐	2	3	1
14	☐	3	1	2
15	☐	2	1	3

Add up all the numbers for the total score and record it on the total score line.

TOTAL SCORE   _____

Now, record how many questions out of 15 were answered

NUMBER OF QUESTIONS   _____

Now, divide the total score by the number of questions answered
Record this final score

FINAL SCORE   _____

Then read the scale to determine your newborn's temperament

SCALE

A rating of 1.0 or close to it would indicate a totally mellow, laid-back newborn.

A rating of 3.0 or close thereto would indicate a very high-strung, intense newborn.

A rating between 1.0 and 2.0 would suggest that the baby is more mellow than high-strung and intense.

A rating between 2.0 and 3.0 would suggest that the baby is more high-strung and intense than mellow.

A rating around 2.0 would indicate that your infant is in the middle of the spectrum of temperament.

To understand the individual aspects of your own newborn's temperament, the following information may be helpful. Questions 1, 5, 9, and 15 evaluate your infant's response to sensory input. Questions 2 and 6 evaluate your baby's output or expression and its intensity. Questions 3, 7, 10, 11, 12, 13, and 14 evaluate your newborn's frustration tolerance or intolerance. Questions 4 and 8 measure your infant's activity level.

Temperament and Height The research on human temperament is in its beginnings and a great deal remains unknown, especially regarding newborn temperament. Temperament is thought to be genetically determined, but influenced by nurturing. Several observations support this. First, you can breed for it in the animal kingdom. Clearly a difference exists between the loveable, extraordinarily friendly black Labrador retriever and the high-strung, "temperamental" German shepherd. Second, human identical twin studies, perhaps, offer the most confirming data supporting the genetic origins of temperament. Studies show that, when identical newborn twins are totally isolated by being separately adopted, they continue to share (regardless of how they are brought up) temperament qualities. Third, temperament is present at birth and tends to endure throughout development and, indeed, for the rest of one's life. Fourth (a little theory of mine), when the genes for temperament are eventually mapped, I would wager that the major gene for temperament will be located on the same chromosome right next to, and linked to, the gene determining height.

Most tall infants, children, and adults that I know tend to be laid-back, easy going, calm, and not easily upset. (Exceptions obviously occur, but are less common and could be explained by genetic "crossover.") Tall newborns, in my experience, tend to be mellow. Tall people have an "even temperament." They are mellow, laid-back. You almost have to stomp on their foot five or six times before they even begin to get upset. And even then, they look at you and query, what are you doing that for?

Whereas many, but not all, short people tend to have a high energy level and are often very expressive of their frustrations just like the high-strung newborn temperament. Perhaps the "Napoleonic complex" is genetic and linked to height as opposed to a reaction from an "inferiority complex" regarding small stature? More often than not, you only have to slightly tweak a short person to see them become seriously upset.

Delight in All Temperaments All types of temperament have positive aspects. The only problem with the high-strung temperament is that parents must wait just a little bit of time to enjoy it.

Within the spectrum of temperament, some newborns, who are initially somewhat high-strung, completely calm themselves down around three and a half months of age as they develop dominance over those initial newborn reflexes. Others, while they gain control over the reflexes and calm themselves down, will remain demanding, expressive, and frustration-intolerant. A small percentage can appear initially mellow but reveal high-strung characteristics at around three weeks of age. With time, these high-strung temperaments adjust and become quite dynamic children and adults, especially if we parents can adapt to them.

For the high-strung temperament, some have understandably used the term "The Difficult Child." Yet, while the high-strung infant is difficult for some parents, he or she is an appreciated spunky delight to others. Perhaps, therefore, a better name is the "high-strung" or "the challenging child." Subsequently parents can help these children adapt by highlighting the positive aspects of their temperament. These high-strung infants can then eventually become sensitive, expressive and powerful young adults.

But it is difficult sometimes. We recently, in our pediatric practice, had a patient and his parents transfer to us because they, and their insurance company, had just spent $25,000 for three weeks in the hospital seeking causes for serious major colic. All the studies were negative. It was clear within minutes of observation that this now four-month-old infant was simply intensely high-strung. The mother gave him a score of almost three on our TENP temperament scales.

53

"Isn't there one right way?"

CHAPTER VII

Others React

FAMILY EXPECTATIONS

Family Expectations (continued, Part II)

I remember my first reaction when the baby was delivered. I was there, and she came out. Well, I had some feeling hoping that this would be a son. But then, it is really is not very…you know,…it wouldn't have made any difference to me either way, but well.

Now the wife of my brother is pregnant. Again, this same crazy pressure is building up for them. I can sense it. My mother keeps saying, "Well, he has three daughters and now he needs a son."

Grandparents and other relatives can have expectations of you and your new baby that can put undue, not to mention unrealistic, pressure on you. This can complicate and diminish your happiness in accomplishing this rite of passage.

BELITTLING GRANDPARENTS

If grandparents and in-laws are belittling or offer unasked-for critical advice, it can erode the budding fragile confidence of trepid new parents. It might be helpful for parents to remember that unasked-for criticism usually has reasons and motivations behind it that has more to do with the giver's anxiety than something the parent is actually doing wrong. For example, perhaps grandparents may be jealous of the new parent's youth, success, and emerging control over his or her own situation? Perhaps they miss not being new parents themselves; perhaps it reminds them of things that are past and no longer possible? Perhaps they wish they could have done it as well as the new parents are doing it? Perhaps by giving critical advice, with the obvious assumption that they know better, they continue in their role as parents to you? But this then does not allow you to stand on your own two feet as a new parent.

More important, grandparents' anxiety regarding their own childbearing practices and difficulties may be reawakened as they watch you. Also, and perhaps most common, their parents and relatives may have belittled them as new parents. And, like fraternity hazing, the ritual is mindlessly perpetuated. "If I suffered through this, then why shouldn't you?" Whatever the case, hang in there. Don't lose your own self-reliance and confidence.

THE INTRUSION OF
THE EXTENDED FAMILY

Some large extended families can be almost too intrusive for new parents. Many families have close ties. Grandparents, uncles, and aunts may all live very close to each other celebrating many cultural and religious holidays together. So, when a young couple has their first baby, the infant may not be the only intruder into the parents' life of intimacy.

New parents may have to accept the intrusion of the entire wonderful family just after delivery and for many, many weeks thereafter. This may be particularly burdensome if the couple is young and has had only a few months together before the wife becomes pregnant. Pregnancy preoccupies their time and thoughts. Delivery automatically welcomes in all of the congratulating, interested, involved, and advice-giving relatives. A young couple may suddenly realize the amount of time they have had for their own life of intimacy together has become even more unbelievably minute.

CONFLICTING ADVICE

"Isn't there one right way?!"

On top of all the common worries, another anxiety for parents who wish to do well, is the inevitable confusion arising from conflicting recommendations. Advice, both sought for (often out of insecure anxiety and/or in an attempt to determine if previously received advice was correct) and unsolicited, comes from the different doctors, the nurses on various shifts, the nurse hired for help upon return home, the relatives from both sides, and family friends.

Conflict begins in the hospital, just after delivery. Usually, it involves some feeding problems. For example, if a difficulty with the initiation of breast-feeding arises, one nurse will recommend one solution while another will encourage something else. When asked, the doctor will suggest something entirely different from either previous recommendation. His partner, on another hospital visit, may seemingly even conflict with that advice. The relatives from both sides will courteously, and sometimes not so courteously, offer their thoughts for success.

The poor parents are left with more uncertainty than ever before. Often they become furious with the nurses, doctors, relatives, and friends who have so generously proffered only confusion with their varied inconsistencies.

WELL? I KNOW MY DELIVERY WAS NOT AN A, USING DRUGS AND ALL. BUT HOW DID I DO? B? B-? C?

If all goes well, it is so nice to be together. But don't grade yourself if it doesn't work out perfectly. You'll be able to hold him soon.

Coping Concepts for Surviving the Baby Bomb

BONDING ENHANCEMENTS AT DELIVERY

The Father's Presence

Having a father present during the labor and delivery is a tremendous enhancement which has only occurred in recent years (*See The Brass Bars*). Now many physicians and hospitals allow fathers to be present, even for emergency Cesarean sections. It is a special thrill for us. It used to be, and still is in many cases, that fathers had little involvement with the new infant until about eight months of age. Being present at delivery involves us fathers much earlier in sharing with our wives the pretty tough, but rewarding, task of bringing life into the world.

Holding and Breast Feeding

If all goes well at birth, it is so nice to be able to hold the baby after delivery. If a mother can also breast-feed then it may add to the closeness. But it is important to realize that if unable to do this, for whatever reason, close bonding will take place regardless of whatever difficulties occur and even if the infant is formula-fed.

Eye Care

To prevent certain causes of blindness, state laws require that the newborn's eyes must be treated with an anti-infection agent just after delivery. These agents cause temporary blurring of vision and puffiness of the lids. Your baby may not open his eyes for a few days. Many parents are, therefore, requesting: (1) that they hold and look at their infant before the treatment, and (2) that less irritating erythromycin eye ointment be used rather than silver nitrate drops.

Rooming-in

The majority of hospitals nowadays offer "partial" rooming-in where the baby stays with the mother in her room during most of the day and evening. The parents, as a consequence, have lots of time to be with their new infant. "Full" rooming-in, with the infant in the room around the clock, is often dependent on the availability of a private room. "Full" rooming-in can also be exhausting and demanding for a mother who has just gone through a significant labor and delivery.

Early Discharge

If the baby and mother are healthy and no complications exist, then leaving as early as possible may be a good idea, for some. Despite all attempts to make it so (many of which are coming quite close to success), the hospital is usually not a place of intimacy. The mother and infant are awakened and checked around the clock. The nurse arouses you for your blood pressure and temperature, the dietician constantly comes for your menu, and the photographer wakes you for baby pictures. None of this mentions the never-ending visits of the obstetrician, the pediatrician, and the relatives.

At home you are in your own comfortable surroundings. It is quiet and peaceful. You may get more rest and have more calm time with your new infant. If mother and infant are home a father will have more time with the new arrival because he will be commuting less between home and the hospital. Also, visitors and relatives can now be scheduled, unlike the hospital where they can just pop in unannounced.

The Importance of Sensuality!

I personally feel that one of the most, if not the most, fundamental aspect of attachment and bonding is sensuality. That's not sexuality, but sensuality. The warm touching, the soothing caressing, and the gentle calming closeness are the adhesives of attachment, longed for by both parents and infant. The sensual holding, smelling, kissing, hugging, nuzzling, and even the endearing soft sounds expressed and heard between parent and child is the extraordinarily important *sine qua non* for attachment and bonding. Sensuality is the glue of attachment! Indeed, it is hard to imagine bonding at all if a child never touched the parents.

Grandparents' Support and Pride

When the entire family, including grandparents, is thrilled with the arrival of a grandchild, it is a very special feeling for the parents. This support positively reinforces the parents' feelings for managing the care of their new baby by themselves. In addition, if the grandparents live close by, they may be able to offer some of their time in caring for the infant.

Soothing, What Is It?

Food and Warmth Soothing is the major empathetic parental function for easing a child's mastery of the relentless frustration innate in all of his development. The type of parental soothing offered varies with what is necessary because of the infant's temperament, his age, our expectations (i.e., our own thoughts regarding what we wish our infant to become like), and our ability to adapt and to sooth based on our own childhood experiences.

60

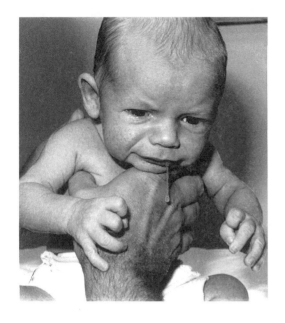

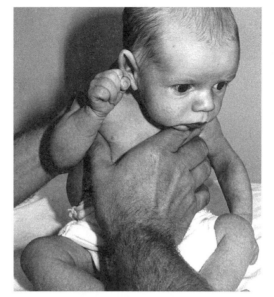

Calming with feather-like, goose-bump raising touch.

*(left)
An irritable, high-strung newborn.*

*(right)
Soothed by gently touching his back.*

Initially, while some newborns are delightfully self-calming, the comforting of others who are high-strung can be totally dependent upon us. Regardless of temperament type, all infants at various times need encouragement, empathic calming, and soothing.

Obviously newborns need soothing by satisfaction of their needs for hunger and warmth. However, they also strive for and more often demand control over their own exasperating reflexes and intense feelings and expressions (i.e. crying perhaps screaming expressions of discomfort). The newborn startle reflex, the uncomfortable but common sensations of parents' cold hands, or even the required movements of a simple diaper replacement, not to mention a bath, may drive early infants crazy, especially if they are on the high-strung side. It quickly becomes apparent that other calming techniques besides feeding and warmth are necessary. A list of the newborn calming methods is presented below.

Talking to Them Most interestingly, newborns have been shown to respond to your consoling facial expressions and comforting tone of voice. You can actually converse

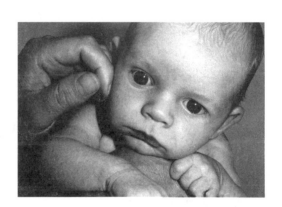

And caressing of the cheeks.

61

with them, and they quiet down and listen! You can talk them down when they are upset! You can empathize with their concerns and they will then calm themselves down — with your help!

Touch Newborns will also react to a very intriguing calming technique: Touch.

Any gentle soothing touch will do, but one of the best is a caressing, feather-light, delightfully goose-bump-raising type of touch. It is best if performed on the back and upper arms along with gentle caressing of the cheeks and chin. The supported newborn then will sit quiet and still, often appearing mesmerized.

SURVIVING THE INTRUDER COMPLEX USING THE PATERNAL INSTINCT

For the father, the newborn becomes real with birth. Initially, fathers are engulfed with a sense of pride for such a miraculous accomplishment. Then, close physical contact follows. Almost every father experiences the deep, strong thrill when the infant quietly snuggles safely and securely on his chest. It is a special feeling to watch him fall asleep there, contentedly, with his little head to one side, his knees drawn up, and his tiny clenched fists held closely to his body and next to yours. A feeling of strength comes over a father when he is able to successfully sooth his infant.

The resolution of the Intruder Complex also comes with the father's strong attachment to his infant.

Thus, the resolution to The Intruder Complex also comes with the father's strong attachment to his new infant. It evolves when the very powerful protective-possessive instincts emerge and the father incorporates the growing reality of the infant into his own sense of self. He then becomes possessive and protective of his new infant. He emerges strong. Many fathers express it thus: "It is really strange. For the first time, I can understand how someone could actually kill to protect his wife or child if they were threatened with real harm."

SURMOUNTING GLITCHES

Dealing With the "Grading System"

As described above, parents and others grade themselves in how well they perform this rite of passage called delivery. They subtract for minor things like: Did I require medication? Or was there a Cesarian section instead of a vaginal delivery? Did I cry? Did I scream?

But the true passage through this rite is maturely handling the cards you are dealt, standing on your own feet being happy with that which goes well and dealing with complications and challenges as they come. That is maturity, and others will deeply respect you for managing it.

Delivery Complications

If the baby, or mother, has problems and is unable to be held just after delivery, it is difficult for parents who yearn to hold their new infant for the first time. It is helpful to take pictures of the baby to keep and look at until you are able to hold him. Most hospitals arrange for this as soon as you can get out of bed and walk to the newborn intensive care unit. There you can scrub your hands and then reach into the incubator to touch.

A mother may have had premature labor and/or a prolonged forced bed-rest prior to delivery. She may then, understandably, have some quite angry feelings toward this new arrival who has "incarcerated" her, often times for months. She may then be reluctant to breast-feed, feeling this attachment at the breast as a further confinement. It helps to share those feelings out loud with your spouse and/or doctor. They will understand. Just the expression and sharing often offers significant relief. To have and express anger is normal.

Cesarian sections

After a Cesarian section, intravenous fluids are dripping into the mother's arm. Her abdomen is sore. Pain medications may make her groggy. Sometimes, with a Cesarian section, the infant must be whisked away to have the mucus sucked from his nose and wind pipe. A mother may not be able to hold and suckle him right after delivery.

In addition, it is not easy to spend as much time with the infant and hold him as close as the mother might wish. If this is the case, two positions are helpful for resolving it. Lying down propped slightly on your side with your baby parallel and facing you, snuggled on a pillow, is one helpful position. Another is to sit propped up in the hospital bed with the baby on two or three pillows in your lap. (See The Emergency Cesarian section)

Resolving the Question: Should I Breast-Feed?

Breast-feeding should be encouraged. It is natural and healthy. It offers some protection for the mother from breast cancer. It helps avoid food allergies in the baby. It also mutes the expression of certain viral illnesses that infants contract. Regarding this last point, breast-feeding is economical if a mother is working. She and/or Dad will probably have to take fewer days off from work. The breast milk is partially protective against some of these viruses and the child, if infected, may show less symptoms of the illness. However, in certain cases, breast-feeding may be risky, such as if a mother is chronically infected with certain viruses or on particular medications.

Given the above, the fundamental question in making the decision for most mothers in developed countries is, "What will enhance my relationship with my baby?" If you feel that breast-feeding will add to the closeness, then go for it. On the other hand, you may perceive that it will detract from the relationship. For example, you may feel it will create a serious resentment on your part. You, after carefully considering the pros and cons, may decide that breast-feeding will be a problem. Then, understandably, it may not be worth the effort.

Many mothers are wary of trying because they might fail. But many are willing to at least try. It is for you to decide. And, no matter what you decide or what happens, don't worry about grading yourself. There are many understandable reasons to breast-feed or not to breast-feed. It is your personal decision to make.

63

Managing the Intruding Extended Family

Many new parents welcome the congratulating extended family. But at times, particularly if a new mother is not feeling well, it is too much. If that is the case, then don't feel guilty about turning off the phone occasionally. Or, if you can afford it, buy an answering machine. Protect yourself so you can enjoy the baby and survive the initial whirlwind. Explain to the others, they will understand…usually.

Hiring a Surrogate Grandmother?

Some affluent parents may consider hiring a baby nurse to help out upon arrival home from the hospital. This baby nurse would take the traditional place of the mother's mother coming to aid with the household duties and child care while the mother recuperates. However, these baby nurses, just like grandmothers, may add or detract from the mother's confidence in herself. Sometimes they are helpful and supportive. Sometimes they may want to impress you with their experience. Sometimes they end up offering unwanted advice or, indeed, taking control of the situation at a time when you want to be with your infant. So it is wise to find out from previous employers what their experience was with this particular baby nurse. Currently many mothers find it much more helpful, obviously if financially feasible, to hire a cleaning person or ask a relative to handle the house, while they themselves care for the infant. Many fathers are able to nowadays take paternity leave and care for the house and help in the care of this new baby. You may find it nice to just be alone at home as a family together.

The cuddler: what everyone dreams for…but not what everyone gets.

ADJUSTMENT TO TEMPERAMENT

Why Discuss Temperament?

If a parent knows little or nothing about the beauty of the variations of temperaments, and receives a newborn with a challenging "high-strung" disposition different from what was expected, then a serious mismatch may follow. Many parents in this situation may lack the knowledge or experience in coping with the "high-strung" type of temperament.

On the other hand, one mother who was a high-powered executive received a beautiful cuddly little girl for whom anyone else would have sold their soul to the devil. Yet this mother was depressed that she had not been delivered a feisty "live-wire." A mismatch cannot only be very upsetting, but it can be the source of poor bonding (particularly for adopting parents) and later serious psychological problems.

The reason that temperament is brought up at all is that if parents are dreaming for a wonderfully cuddly mellow baby and they receive one, then fine. However, if we are anticipating a mellow infant and deliver (or adopt) a spirited, high-strung baby who is quite different from our expectations, conflicts joltingly arise. If we know how to enhance the strength and character of this high-strung infant then we can bond and enhance his strengths. The only problem is that we may have to wait a few months to enjoy them.

The Apparently Rejecting Baby

A newborn can look beyond us at the whole spectrum of his environment. He may ignore our eyes and look at all aspects of the periphery around our heads. This early lack of eye contact can feel like a rejection of our best efforts to engage him. We can become angry and retaliate. An understanding of this phenomenon helps parents accept the newborn's sometimes curious, but apparently insensate behavior. It only takes about six weeks for him to become focused on you.

Calming Techniques for Babies, Especially the High-strung

Even after understanding that the high-strung newborn can eventually be a delight, parents can be profoundly perplexed, if not furious, in their failed attempts to calm this infant. Below are some of the calming techniques useful for the high-strung infant. These methods help also in calming the upset mellow baby.

1. Swaddling. (see photo on page 48) Swaddling for the newborn has been used in all cultures for century upon century. To swaddle is to completely wrap the baby tightly in "receiving" blankets so that only his head is exposed. This helps the baby abort the startle reflex. When his hands

are free and flailing about with the uncontrollable startle-cry reflex, he is incapable of calming himself down.

To swaddle, place a receiving blanket like a diamond in front of you. Fold the top of the diamond down about five inches. Place the baby on the blanket with the back of his neck at the fold so that his head is just above and not on the blanket. While holding his left arm along his side, tightly wrap that corner of the blanket over his left arm around his torso and under his right arm and back so that it is caught between the blanket and his back. Bring the bottom corner up to the level of his chin to enclose his feet. Then, while holding the baby's right arm snug against his body, tightly bring the remaining right corner over this arm, around and behind the baby's left arm to firmly enclose and secure the infant in the blanket. It is also helpful to have a second light blanket folded like a rectangle to further wrap around the swaddled newborn to secure the first swaddling blanket. Ask the nurses in the hospital to show you how to do it before you leave.

Some parents worry that swaddling may be restrictive and cruel. But, in fact, swaddling is organizing for the hyper-reflexive newborn. It allows the baby to concentrate on intentional activity without the disruptive, distracting non-volitional reflex behavior. If an infant's arms are flying about with the startle reflex, then it is very difficult to concentrate on suckling. Also, if the arms are flailing about, then simply looking around to discover and concentrate on the environment is extremely difficult. Swaddling is not cruel, it is comforting — for the newborn.

65

2. Soothing Touch. Feathery, goose-bump-raising touch is often a forgotten calming technique as parents seek to hug and snuggle. See the illustrations on page 61 for techniques and their effect.

3. Smooth Motion. Movement is often helpful, but should be employed with the intent to console. Some caretakers may anxiously jostle the baby up and down, like a woodpecker's pecking. This can over-stimulate the hypersensitive, hyper-reflexive newborn and often cause even more crying. Infants can feel the tenseness in the parent's muscles. On the other hand, walking with the baby in a carriage or stroller is soothing for both parent and child. A drive in the car will often put the infant to sleep. A baby swing, while initially or sometimes calming, may irritate the infant with the clicking noise. But, it is worth a try. Walking, with its calming and rhythmic rocking, is comforting for the baby in your arms or on your shoulder. Some old-fashioned infant cribs will rock, but again, the squeaky noise and hard mattress can be upsetting. Some parents have found, suprisingly, that putting the infant in the car seat and placing that on the turned-on clothes washer or dryer is very effective.

The calming of motion and sucking.

An occasional infant furniture store may carry a safe hammock for the high-strung infant. Quiet motion, along with the snuggled close feeling of the enclosed hammock, can be very comforting. Some hammock-like infant seats, particularly those from Europe, are designed to gently rock as the baby begins to move, startle and cry.

4. Being on His Stomach. A high-strung infant is often happier when placed, during the day, on his stomach on the floor, playpen, or crib. If placed on his back, he feels as if he is falling and will flail about as the startle-cry reflex begins. However, being on his stomach forces him to lift his head and that, in itself, may be difficult and quite frustrating. So no matter what position you place him in, you may need to allow him to master his frustration when faced with these little, but for him, tough tasks. Remember, however, that actual sleeping on the back, during the night and for daytime naps, is safer and protects against Sudden Infant Death Syndrome.

5. Placing a High-strung Newborn. When it is necessary to place a hypersensitive baby on his back for cleaning and changing, it can be done in a calming manner. This is performed like a judo rolling fall. While the infant is still cradled in your arms, slowly turn him on his left side, holding both of his hands together against his chest. While still on his side and in your arms, tilt his head and left shoulder down toward the surface of the changing table. Lower him so that just the head and shoulder touch the table. Then lower the rest of him to the table as you simultaneously roll him on to his back. Continue holding his hands together against his chest under his chin during the entire maneuver.

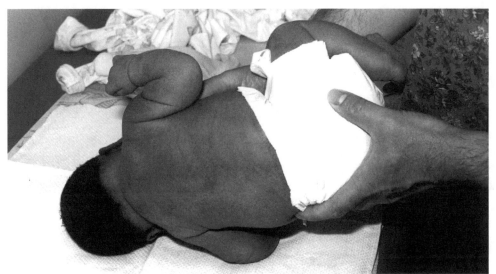

(a)

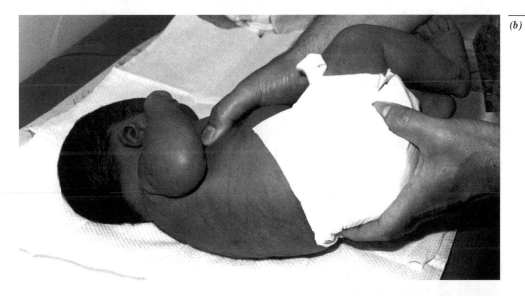

(b)

Technique No. 5.

The judo roll: a calming way to set a high-strung newborn down. (a) His head and shoulders touch the mattress first as you hold his diapered rear with one hand and his chest with your other hand. (b) Then roll him gently onto his back. (c) Notice he has not startled yet. If he does, just hold his hands together and let him suck on your upside-down little finger (see calming technique No. 7).

67

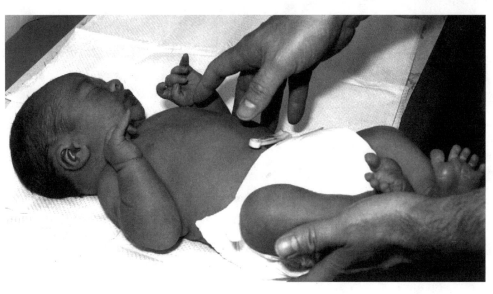

(c)

6. Sitting With Support. Frustration intolerant infants often do not like being held upright either in your hands or close to your chest. Their chest falls on the stomach and their head clunks down or around making it sometimes difficult to breathe. That is what makes airplane-ing (see below) so comfortably soothing. But another method of holding them is portrayed below. Notice (1) your thumb supports one armpit while the middle or fourth finger is under the other armpit leaving the index finger, or the knuckle of the index finger, to prop up the chin. This is also a great posture for burping and for the feathery soothing touch of his back.

68

Technique No. 6.

A calming method to support him upright. Note the thumb of the supporting left hand is under the infant's left armpit. The ring finger braces up the right armpit while the index finger or its knuckle props the chin up. All of this occurs while your right hand supports his back.

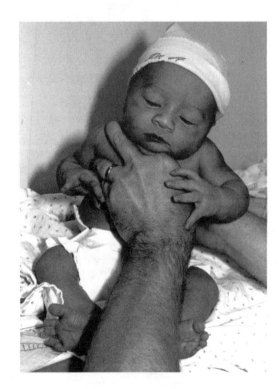

(a)

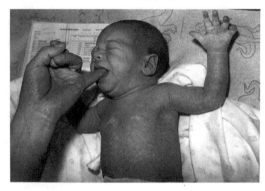

(b)

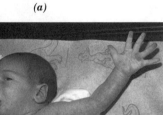

(c)

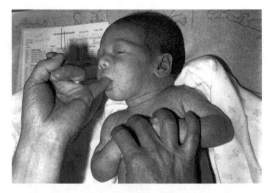

Technique No. 7.

Stopping the startling. (a) A newborn will suck on your little finger upside down. (b) But if he startles, he loses his concentration on his intentional suck. (c) If you hold his hands together to prevent the distracting startle reflex, he can more easily reinitiate intentional sucking.

7. Preventing the Distracting, Upsetting Startle Reflex. The newborn frequently wants to suck on your finger or pacifier, but is unable to concentrate on that motion because he is being jerked about by his other reflex movements. A helpful technique, when swaddling is not feasible, is to hold the infant's hands together against the chest under their chin while offering your little finger upside down against the roof of the mouth. It may be necessary to gently and calmly move your finger around inside the mouth to stimulate saliva production and the sucking reflex. When successful sucking begins, the infant's shoulders will arch forward with arms flexed pulling at your grip.

If his hands break free, he will startle and be unable to suck until calmed down again. When that occurs simply try again with a stronger hold of his hands against the chest.

8. Rubbing Out the Frown. A true forehead frown is often seen even though you are holding his hands against his chest in a calming position. Without letting go of his hands, you may be able to gently rub the frown off his forehead by moving your thumb and forefinger across the brow. This is often comforting and will relieve his tension and frustration.

9. Avoid Startling Noises. Have a quiet, soothing nursery or setting. Loud television sets or clocks can upset the high-strung infant. The loud, anxious, repetitive noises that some of us make with our mouth while jostling him up and down can be over-stimulating. These sounds and shakes appear to arise from our attempts to stop his incessant crying. If we jostle and frighten him enough

he must catch his breath during the startle reflex's quiet-fright phase, occurring just before their scream with arms thrusting out. Also, if we do it enough, he may perhaps exhaust himself. Avoid blowing in his face for the same reasons. While it will cause them to stop crying for an instant, it is always followed by startled, more intense cries.

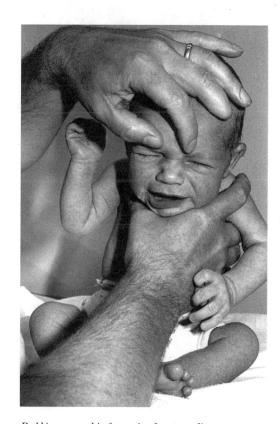

Rubbing away his frown is often consoling.

69

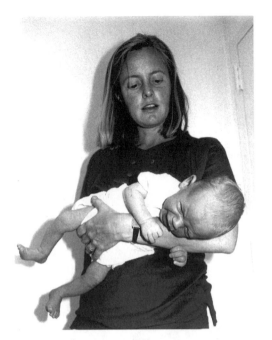 

Airplane-ing: the most successful calming technique. (a) Just starting the airplane-ing. (b) The calm has arrived.

10. "Airplane-ing." One of the most successful calming techniques discovered by parents is "airplane-ing." The infant is held like a football placed stomach side down on the parent's forearm. The parent's hand is supporting the infant's body by holding the diaper at the crotch. The infant's head is on the outside of the parent's elbow. The infant's arm and leg on one side are held between the parent's arm and trunk. The other arm and leg dangle free on the outside of the parent's forearm. The infant can then be glided, gently not nervously, back and forth through the air on the forearm of the parent's rotating body using the motion of the dance called the "twist." The baby feels secure in this position and does not experience the sensation of falling. Also, while held in this calming position, he loves to look out and down at all the interesting items around him. Sometimes, it is also soothing for the parent to use their free hand to gently rub the infant's back while rotating the infant in this position. Addi-

tionally, the little finger or thumb of the free hand can be used to let the infant suck on. This position is more often discovered by fathers. It is not as satisfying to a mother who wants to hold the baby snuggled close and facing her body.

To get in this position, hold the baby on your chest but facing out away from you. Hold onto one thigh near the hip with your one hand which is also supporting his bottom (Step 1). Take your other hand to his opposite shoulder trapping his arm against you. Then with that hand reach deep down into his diapered crotch (Step 2) while he gently leans over to rest on your forearm (Step 3). Then, if more calming is needed, take the now free hand that was holding his bottom and thigh and go between his legs (Step 4) snagging the baby's free arm (to keep it from being involved in a startle reflex) and insert your thumb as a pacifier upside down in the roof of his mouth up to the bottom of your thumb nail while holding onto his free hand (Step 5).

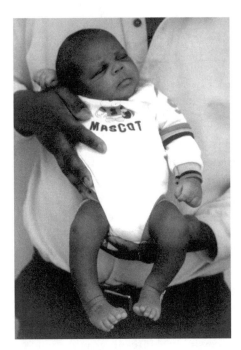

Step 1

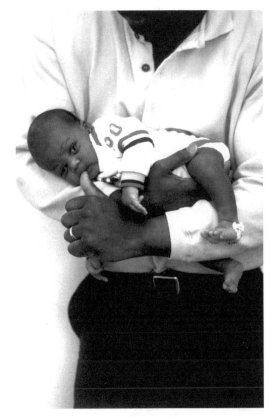

*How to get into
the Airplane-ing
position.*

Step 4

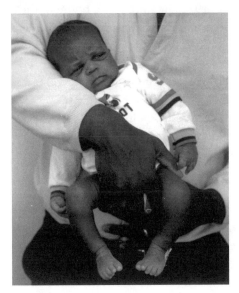

Step 2

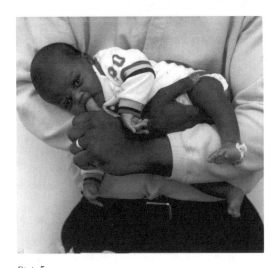

Step 5

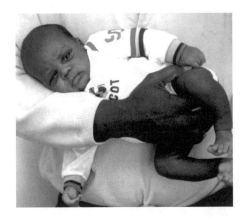

Step 3

11. The Window and The Walk. The window and walking are often so intriguing that the high-strung infant is captured by curiosity. His attention to newness, as he peers out the window of your home or looks about during a walk, stuns his body to stillness. He relaxes, especially if held in the "airplane-ing" position, and gazes out at this brand new world beyond.

Breast-Feeding the High-strung Newborn

"When he cries, I cry. It's hard, very hard." In my experience, the high-strung newborn temperament is the most common cause of breast-feeding failure. These newborns are so jerked around by their startle reflex that they are unable to concentrate on sucking. They also often have a jaw clamp as part of their hyper-reflexiveness. These two reflexes prevent them from voluntarily opening their mouth and attaching to the nipple of the breast. When they try to get the nipple, the jaw may not be able to open because of the jaw-clamp reflex and then their whole body-startle may fling them back and away from the breast thereby making calm, intentional sucking very difficult. In addition, when hungry and unable to attach, their frustration-intolerance takes over, causing them to arch back. Thus they give the appearance of rejecting the breast, scream, and go into yet another frustrating startle reflex which makes it impossible for them to concentrate on attaching and sucking.

Unfortunately, it is much easier to bottle feed these infants and to use a pacifier to calm them. The nipple of the bottle or pacifier can be forced between and past the lips and gums which are clenched together by the jaw reflex. They are then quickly gratified with their ability to suck, thus relieving their screaming frustration. If this takes place, it becomes very difficult, sometimes impossible, to get them back to sucking on the nipple of the breast.

If successful breast feeding is the goal, then these infants should never be given a pacifier or see the nipple of a bottle in the first three-to-four weeks of life. If they need to be pacified, then they can learn to suck on the crooked knuckle of your little finger. The crooked knuckle can be gently forced past the clinched jaw. This technique teaches them how to relax their jaw while they learn the proper suck, since that required for the knuckle is comparable to the suck necessary for the breast. If this type of infant needs either supplemental fluids or nourishment, then it can be given by a small medicine cup or a needleless syringe placed at the corner of the mouth. This requires no sucking. Also, when breast feeding they need to be very well swaddled so that they can't startle and be distracted from learning to suck.

Another important point is to learn how to hold the baby in the cradle position with only one arm with the hand of that arm behind the baby's head (see photo on page 39 for example). That way when he throws himself back you can hold him forward to keep him focused on sucking the nipple. It also frees up your opposite hand so that you can use it to press down on your breast right above the baby's nose so that the breast does not obstruct his breathing through his nose. When suckling, babies are obligate nose breathers. If they can't breathe while sucking, they understandably pull off, and back, to catch their breath.

Breast-feeding the high-strung newborn is extremely hard on the mother who is usually expecting an exhilarating and successful experience. The infant can appear unhappy and rejecting, and this is hard on the mother: "When he cries, I cry. It is hard, very hard." It is helpful, when this happens, to know that it is the newborn's temperament, and not any inability of the mother that is causing the conflict. Realizing that this temperament has benefits down the road is comforting. But the loss of this longed-for, blissful experience is extraordinarily difficult. What the mother had wished for and was dreaming about during pregnancy did not come true.

But if you truly persist, and this type of infant is not exposed to bottle nipples or pacifiers, successful breast-feeding will be established within one to three weeks. Ask your pediatrician for further help.

WISH VERSUS REALITY REVISITED

"Well, I got a little bit more than I had bargained for."

A mother who had just delivered a high-strung newborn, understatedly uttered, "Well, I got a little bit more than I had bargained for." A common early conflict of "Wish Versus Reality" comes after delivery, when the infant's temperament is sometimes different from our expectations. If any drastic difference occurs from what a parent's expectations are, then an emotional adjustment must be made. During this time an actual mourning process can become very apparent. The most common mismatch leading to this conflict occurs when a mother anticipating a "quiet, sweet cuddler" receives instead the high-strung frustration-intolerant newborn.

Going Home Without the Present

Mothers have the wish and longing to go home with their baby on the second or third hospital day. However, if the reality of marked jaundice, or some other problem, intrudes and requires continued hospitalization for the baby, it can be truly saddening for the parents who were counting on going home with their new baby. It's like having a birthday party without receiving any presents. See page 28 for the solution.

Resolving "Isn't There One Right Way?"

When confronted with conflicting advice as described above (See Conflicting Advice on page 56 and also see Hiring a Surrogate Grandmother? on page 64), it is wise to dissect out how this happened. The solution: Stick to one chef, your pediatrician. I have no wish to be sententious, but remember, "Too many cooks spoil the broth." Also remember that there are many different ways to make lasagna. In other words, many different approaches can solve the same problem. But, it is wise to systematically go through them under the guidance of one knowledgeable chef. That way you can try different tactics sequentially. In this manner, you can learn what is best for you and your situation with less anxiety. It is not that one chef is right and the others are wrong. It is

73

THE SWEET TEMPERMENT IS MINE BUT THAT NOSE COMES FROM YOUR MOTHER!

rather that there are different strategies, all of which may be correct. But, if presented or sought after all at one time, they may become quite confusing to new and anxious parents.

Resolving "Wish Versus Reality" Conflicts

"How could this happen to me? I did everything right during the pregnancy."

Parents, when confronted with "Wish Versus Reality" conflicts, need to assess what is going on. Do they feel the need to control the situation, even when nature has taken it out of their control? Do they feel entitled?

How could this happen to me? When thrust into this situation, it is better to adapt to the reality than to persist in wishing for something beyond it. One does what one can, and then one must acclimate. The only decent thing about suffering trauma is that it strengthens us so that we can later on savor the good things that eventually happen.

**THE HUMOR OF...
NARCISSISTIC REJECTION**

One father smilingly joshed, "He gets his looks from my side and his bad temper from your side of the family."

A humorous feeling occurs in almost every parent that "his looks are mine, but his temper is yours" or "his sweet temperament is from my side but that nose is from yours." We reject the unpleasant or disagreeable parts as belonging to someone other than ourselves and our side of the family, while we claim the grand and glorious attributes of the child as coming from ourselves.

In the Greek myth, Narcissus was condemned by an avenging goddess to fall in love with his own image reflecting back to him from a crystal clear fountain. All of us appreciate ourselves, our heritage, family, and our genes. We like to think that all the positive qualities of our offspring belong to us and our family. However, anything negative we just might reject, thinking or wishing it came from elsewhere. Where else? The other side.

When feeling this, it is nice to remind ourselves of our togetherness, our love, and of what we the parents committed to with our wedding vows. Remember those? We chose each other and pledged to "...for better or for worse, and in sickness and in health..." Sticking together makes enjoying this wonderful new baby even better.

Most of the time these narcissistic expressions are simply humorous comments reflecting our identification with our newborn while poking a little fun at in-laws. Infrequently, just as for Narcissus, they can represent ill-concealed manifestations of a curse: If a parent becomes angry with a spouse and feels the desire to truly reject the new baby as not in any way his or hers, or not at all like me, then that is a serious obstacle. "This is your baby, not mine!" Professional help to deal with this problem should be sought as soon as it is recognized. At the very least, think of all the good qualities that convinced you to marry this other side.

ADOPTION

Narcissistic Rejection and Temperament

When expecting any new baby, adopting parents (like all other expecting parents) are usually dreaming of the mellow laid-back newborn as described above in the discussion on temperament. If, by chance, adopting parents have thrust upon them a high-strung, hyper-reflexive, shrill-crying newborn, it is difficult...often very difficult.

It comes from the "birth mother." They think this temperament has nothing to do with them the adopting parents. Bonding thus can become very difficult: it is hard to put up with the seeming rejection of this infuriated, screaming and high-strung new-

born. "He didn't get this from me." "This is not what I dreamt about." (See Resolving Wish Versus Reality Conflicts, page 74.)

Just as with any birth, with adoption you cannot always predict what you will receive. And what you receive may differ from what you were dreaming of. It is best to be maturely prepared for this fact ahead of time. This helps you to accept what comes. Then from there use your nurturing and caring handling of him to help him adapt to the world while you adapt to him. Studies are showing that nurturing is far more important than we thought. The high-strung infant will become a delightful challenge and a wonderful adult. But in the beginning we must adapt to him and not ask him to be different from what he is. (See temperament above)

Touch and Bond

Unbelievable new research is emerging. It shows that a major aspect of bonding and attachment is actually biochemical. It appears that hormones may be released in the interactions between infant and parents, and these hormones apparently hit or attach to certain centers in the brains of infants and parents. The most important interaction is perhaps touch. It is the soothing, caressing, calm fondling, kissing, and nuzzling that glues parents to their infant and the infant to the parents. It releases goose-bump raising hormones. It ties the bond.

This touching creates the bond of intimacy between parents and infant. If parents adopt late, then to regress to carrying the infant around held closely, and then

75

progressing from there, is beneficial. Some adopting mothers find breast-feeding, not necessarily for nourishment, a warm and close experience. For either parent, taking a bath with the new baby in the early months can enhance the closeness. To ensure bonding, warm and loving touch and closeness is always encouraged.

HELPING THE OLDER SIBLING SURVIVE

Obviously attempt, when possible, to prepare the older one for the new arrival as outlined in Chapter IV. This clearly is not possible in all instances. Some parents not being raised in a thoughtful mode by their own parents do not have the repertoire to

An older brother's unbelievable sense of loss, "Why wasn't I enough?!"

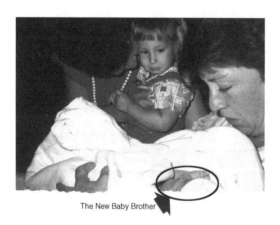

The New Baby Brother

think of such things. Others have been caught up in certain extraneous circumstances or complications of pregnancy and delivery. They have had, to their own regret, little chance to expedite what they would like to do for the older sibling.

An axiom: When a baby is born who has an older sibling, that older sibling is going to react. Another axiom: The closer the

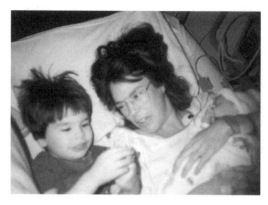

It's caring to bring your older one(s) to the hospital to sit and be with you and the new baby.

attachment of that older sibling to the parents the greater the reactions. The last axiom: The reaction is modulated, to some extent (and only to some extent), by the temperament of the sibling and the thoughtfulness of the parents.

If the sibling is nine months to four and a half years of age, the reaction is more often than not one of sadness as well as seeking negative attention, or keeping you, the parents, on "a short leash." If older, while a sense of loss and anger may simmer undetected in the cauldron, the older sibling feels ostensibly proud and wants to show friends this new doll, this new possession.

Regardless of preparation, after the birth it is caring to bring your older child (children) to the hospital to sit and be with you. It is warm and nice for the older sibling(s) to sit and hold the new one. Teaching the older one(s) to use an open palm for touching in a soft and caring manner, to "make nice," initiates a sibling bond. Also, remember the points already made in Chapter IV. These thoughtful supports for the older sibling begin on page 26.

And now out of the hospital and back to home...for the first six weeks.

Glossary

ANECDOTE: According to Webster's New International Dictionary, an anecdote is "a short narrative of an interesting, amusing, or curious incident often biographical and generally characterized by human interest". That's a perfect description of our use of anecdotes.

ATTACHMENT, BONDING: The process whereby an infant forms an irreversibly intimate relationship with his parents and recognizes them as his and recognizes others as strangers or non-parents. The importance of its necessity and strength cannot be over-estimated; it is critical for the child's security and later on for his own life of intimacy with others. It is an extraordinarily complex process which is poorly understood and takes place even in adoption. It is not as fragile a process as first thought, and minor events which may interfere with closeness will not interfere with successful bonding.

BONDING: See ATTACHMENT, BONDING above.

COLIC (adjective: colicky): Episodes of severe acute abdominal pain in the small infant. They double up squirming and crying. It usually is simply some abdominal discomfort in an infant with the "high-strung", hypersensitive temperament. But there are other causes and it may take a bit of detective work and patience to work it out. Most colic is gone by the age of three and a half months.

ENDOMETRIOSIS: The presense of functioning endometrial tissue (tissue that usually lines the inside of the uterus) in places where it does not belong such as in the pelvic cavity outside the uterus.

FACIAL MASK OF PREGNANCY: The hormones of pregnancy can, in some mothers, cause a dark pigmented rash in a butterfly distribution over the nose and onto the cheeks.

FETUS (Adjective: FETAL): After a sperm and ovum meet, or the ovum is fertilized by the sperm, the fertilized ovum or embryo attaches to the wall of the uterus and grows there. After the first three months or so the growing fertilized egg is no longer called an embryo but is termed a fetus.

79

GASTROCOLIC REFLEX: When food or formula hits the stomach, not only does the stomach start to process it but the entire intestinal tract is activated. Consequently, if stool or gas is in the lower large intestine, it is common to want to pass it. Thus, in the newborn period, it is not uncommon for an infant to start feeding and then, approximately 40-50 seconds later, to arch back and cry with a gaseous cramp and then to even pass stool.

"HIGH-STRUNG" TYPE TEMPERAMENT: An infant with this temperament type is dominated by the newborn reflexes. His high sensitivity to touch and loud noises easily evokes his Moro (see below) startle reflex. His inability to control these reflexes is extraordinarily frustrating for him, and he expresses his frustration with a piercing, angry scream. He is frustration-intolerant unlike his opposite, the "laid-back, mellow" type of temperament. While challenging at first, this type of temperament becomes quite delightful with time.

HYPERSENSITIVE, HYPER-REFLEXIVE: See in this Glossary descriptions for the REFLEX-DOMINATED and the HIGH-STRUNG newborn.

INTIMACY DRIVE, THE: In healthy environments, both parents and newborn infant are literally driven to recognize each other, become close, and evolve toward an intimate relationship. Sensuality is initially the most significant means by which this instinctually driven desire is accomplished. The parents snuggle, caress, and seek eye contact. The infant eventually responds and, when physically capable, dives back into the parents' bodies. This is one of the most powerful and wonderful drives of all animals, including humans.

The closeness of the intimacy drive in an infant imprints for his intimate relationships later in life. As he separates he seeks intimate relationships with others, He seeks close friends. He tries out partners and eventually chooses a spouse for the development of deep intimacy. The Intimacy Drive has now gone full circle.

Along the way mentors are found. The young adult develops intimate trusting relationships with them in order to reach certain aspirations.

The Intimacy Drive is for the first time described in this series. It is stronger than the sex or hunger drives for parents will forgo sex and food for the development of intimacy with their offspring. The conflicts of the Intimacy Drive are Separation issues and The Intruder Complex and sabotage and conditional love, topics which will be dealt with in later books.

Biochemical factors more than likely play an important role in The Intimacy Drive.

INTRUDER COMPLEX, THE: The mixture of feelings in which the parents consciously or unconsciously sense the reality of their new infant's intrusion into their own life of intimacy together. These feelings begin during the pregnancy and persist throughout all of the child's development.

KAMIKAZE MODE: A father will often interact with the infant in a way that appears adventurous. The father may seem disruptive (or Kamikaze) of the usual routine established by the mother. It prepares the child for the aspects of life which are chaotic or competitive. It counterbalances the homeostasis which a mother desires and establishes.

LET-DOWN REFLEX: When a breast feeding infant first attaches to the nipple, a stimulus goes through the mother's nerves up the spinal cord and to the brain, there initiating the secretion of two hormones into the blood stream from the pituitary gland at the base of the brain. One of the hormones tells the breasts to make milk.

The other literally pumps the milk out. That is the so-called "let-down" reflex as the milk comes out. A small microscopic cuff of smooth muscle tissue is present in every duct in the breast. When the hormone hits the muscle, it contracts the muscle and milks the milk out. That hormone also acts on other smooth muscle, namely that of the uterus. So, it is not at all uncommon for breast-feeding mothers to complain of cramps or increased blood flow with nursing in the immediate post-partum period. This also helps the uterus to return to its normal size.

MORO STARTLE REFLEX: The startle reflex of the newborn whereby they look as if they are falling. Their arms fling out in an arched embrace and they have a frightened, startled, and wide-eyed expression on their face. It looks as if they are trying to balance themselves from a fall in space. They do it primarily when tossed into the air or placed on their backs. They tend not to do it on their stomachs because their arms are secured against the mattress or table.

NEONATE: Another word for newborn. A neonatal intensive care unit is an intensive care unit for newborns.

NEWBORN: Any infant under thirty days after delivery.

OBSTETRICIAN: A doctor who is certified to deliver babies and manage all the complications of delivery.

PEDIATRICIAN: A doctor who is trained and certified to handle problems of patients whose ages are from birth through college.

POSTPARTUM: A medical phrase referring to the time just after delivery of a baby.

REFLEX-DOMINATED NEWBORN (see High-strung temperament): The particular type of temperament of a newborn child (1) who is dominated by the newborn reflexes (such as the Moro reflex, see above), (2) who is sensitive to stimuli which set off these reflexes, and (3) who also vehemently expresses his frustration over his lack of control over these reflexes. Dr. Spock called this type of newborn the "hypertonic" newborn. Others have also called him the "jittery" newborn.

REGRESSION: The act or process of behaving much younger than our actual chronological age, e.g. behaving "like a baby."

SIB (Plural form: SIBS): Slang for SIBLING(S).

SIBLING: A brother or a sister.

SIBLING RIVALRY: When a newborn arrives and even before, during the pregnancy, an older brother or sister will resent having to share their mother and father with the new sibling. Their rivalry with the new baby for the mother is often manifested in attention getting behavior such as regressive or younger behavior, for example, wetting or soiling, and/or overt physical aggression toward the younger sibling. As the younger child grows, he too can become rivalrous with the older sibling for his mother's attention.

SINE QUA NON: A Latin phrase for something indispensable, that without which nothing else would exist or occur.

SINUSITIS: An inflammation of the sinuses (the air cavities in the facial bones next to the nose).

SONOGRAM: Sound waves can be bounced off a structure, and the returning reflected waves are then monitored by recording equipment. The reflected wave measurements can be put together to form an image of the structure, and this image can be monitored on a television screen. Sonograms are safely and commonly employed to obtain a picture of the fetus in the womb. Sonography can also be used to harmlessly look at the heart; this is called an echo-cardiogram. Sonography is also extremely valuable for looking at the contents of the abdomen, such as the kidneys and the ovaries.

SONOGRAPHY: See sonogram above. The process of obtaining a sonogram.

SPERM: The motile male reproductive cell produced by the testes which comes out of the penis in the semen during orgasm. When introduced within the vagina, they travel up through the uterus seeking an ovum (the egg released by the ovary). When one finds the ovum, it plunges inside the ovum and fertilizes it.

STARTLE REFLEX: See the above description of the Moro startle reflex.

STOOL: Feces, or the material passed out the anus during the defecation process.

TEMPERAMENT: The probably genetically determined disposition of an infant, child, or for that matter an adult. Parents can develop a reasonably good idea of their infant's temperament soon after birth. The spectrum of temperament ranges from the quiet huggable cuddly laid-back infant to the high-strung hyper-reflexive, hypersensitive, frustration-intolerant newborn.

TENP SCALE: Temperament Evaluation of the Newborn by Peebles scale.

TERM: "Term" is the expression for the end of a normal pregnancy of nine months or forty weeks. "Pre-term" indicates that the infant was born prior to term. Likewise, "post-term" indicates the newborn was born after the usual 40 weeks of gestation.

TRIMESTER: A pregnancy runs nine months under normal circumstances. Each of the three three-month periods of those nine months is called a trimester.

"WISH VS. REALITY": The ever-present conflict in parents whereby our wish for the child or infant does not conform with the reality which the child lives with and presents to us.

83

Index

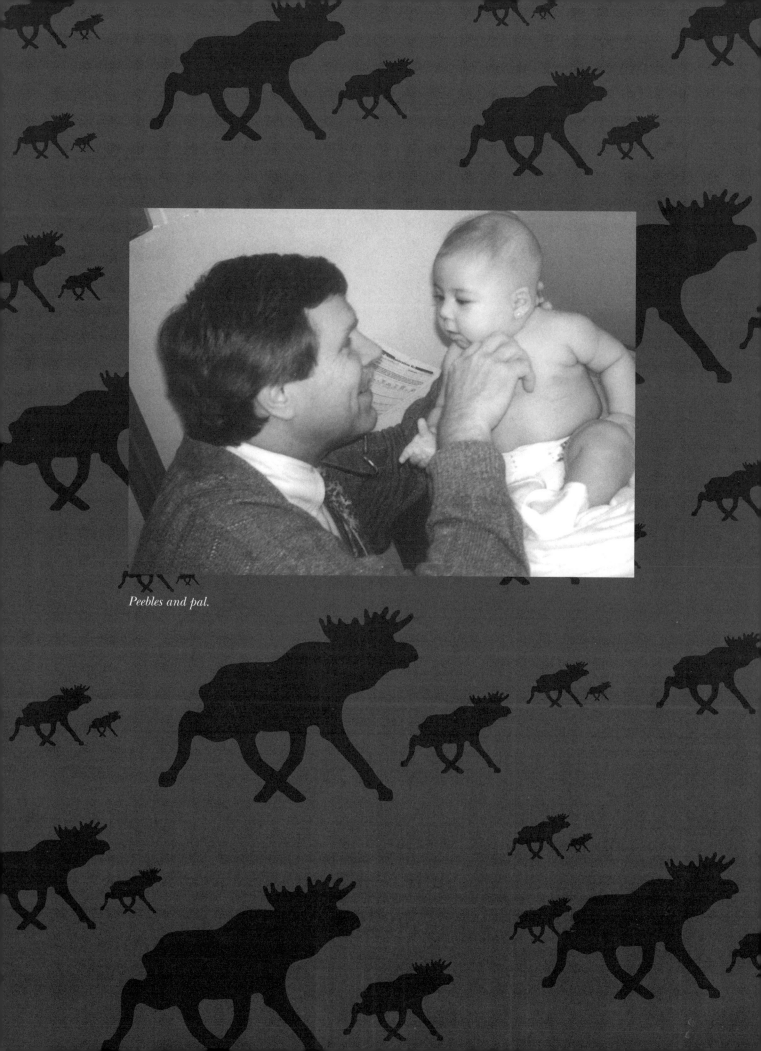

Peebles and pal.

THE AUTHOR

Paul Peebles, a husband and father of two, received his medical degree from Case Western Reserve University and completed his pediatric internship at University Hospitals (Cleveland) where his preceptor was Dr. Benjamin Spock. He fulfilled his residency at Harvard's Children's Hospital Medical Center (Boston) training with Dr. T. Berry Brazelton. Dr. Peebles served as a Clinical Associate, Staff Associate, and Senior Investigator at the National Institutes of Health (Washington, D.C.), and performed additional research at the Karolinska Institute (Stockholm) and at Children's Hospital Medical Center (Boston). He was on the faculty of Harvard University School of Medicine. He is currently a Professor of Pediatrics and Hematology-Oncology at The Johns Hopkins University School of Medicine (Baltimore), Children's National Medical Center of George Washington University's School of Medicine (Washington, D.C.), and at Georgetown University's School of Medicine (Washington, D.C.). Dr. Peebles belongs to eight professional societies, including the prestigious Society for Pediatric Research. He is currently in private practice as Director of The Pediatric Care Center in Bethesda, Maryland. Dr. Peebles is a writer-scientist with many publications including articles with primary authorship published in *Nature* and *Science*. In *The Washingtonian* magazine he has been elected by his peers as "one of the area's leading primary care physicians."

And now, onto the rest of *The Parents' Survival Kit.*

89

NOTES

NOTES

NOTES